THE FAR EDGES OF THE FOURTH GENRE

THE FAR EDGES OF THE FOURTH GENRE

An Anthology of Explorations in Creative Nonfiction

EDITED BY

SEAN PRENTISS AND **JOE WILKINS**

MICHIGAN STATE UNIVERSITY PRESS

East Lansing

⊗

The paper used in this publication meets
the minimum requirements of
ANSI/NISO Z39.48-1992 (R 1997)
(Permanence of Paper).

Michigan State University Press
East Lansing, Michigan 48823-5245

Printed and bound in the United States of America.

20 19 18 17 16 15 14   1 2 3 4 5 6 7 8 9 10

Library of Congress Cataloging-in-Publication Data
The far edges of the fourth genre : an anthology of explorations
in creative nonfiction / edited by Sean Prentiss and Joe Wilkins.
       pages   cm
ISBN 978-1-61186-121-1 (pbk. : alk. paper)— ISBN 978-1-60917-411-8 (ebook)
1. Creative nonfiction—Authorship. 2. Essay—Authorship.
I. Prentiss, Sean editor of compilation. II. Wilkins, Joe editor of compilation.
PN145.F37 2014
808.02—dc23
2013024258

Book design by Walton Harris
Cover design by Shaun Allshouse, www.shaunallshouse.com

Michigan State University Press is a member of the Green Press Initiative and
is committed to developing and encouraging ecologically responsible publishing
practices. For more information about the Green Press Initiative and the use of
recycled paper in book publishing, please visit www.greenpressinitiative.org.

Visit Michigan State University Press at www.msupress.org

To Sarah for sharing my love for creative nonfiction (and for sharing this wonderful life). And always to Mom and Dad. Joe, thanks for joining me on this journey to the edges of creative nonfiction.
 —SEAN PRENTISS

Thanks, Sean, for your vision. This one's for Walter and Edie, my son and daughter, that they know the stories behind them.
 —JOE WILKINS

And our warmest thanks to Molly Waite, our assistant editor, for keeping us on task, for reading every essay with both a writer's and an editor's eye, and for joining us on this adventure deep into the heart of creative nonfiction. Thank you, Molly. We couldn't have done it without you!

And, finally, thanks to all the great authors collected in this anthology. Your ideas on creative nonfiction are what excites us about writing our next essays and our next memoirs.

CONTENTS

INTRODUCTION

As creative nonfiction writers and professors who teach creative nonfiction writing, we've been thinking about how readers and writers often view creative nonfiction as a static genre, a place to tell true stories with standard narrative arcs. Or as a genre that follows in the footsteps of fiction, while sticking (mostly) to fact or truth (whatever they might be). Yet the old adage—and adages often get old and overused for the very elemental bits of wisdom in them—has it that truth is stranger than fiction. Thus, if there are a thousand and one ways to structure a short story, there must be, at least, a thousand and two ways to wend through an essay. If the novel continues to be as vital and mysterious as ever, the memoir, too, must contain unknown, as-of-yet unexplored countries and unmapped landscapes.

And though creative nonfiction has been around since Montaigne's *essais*, St. Augustine's *Confessions*, or Seneca's writings from two thousand years ago, we've noticed during our collective decades of teaching creative nonfiction that there is a hole in the pedagogy. Even though people have been writing creative nonfiction for millennia, we've only begun to ask how this genre works, why it functions the way it does, and where its borders reside. But for each question we ask, for each question that we struggle to answer, another five or ten questions roil to the surface. And it seems that each of these questions requires a more convoluted series of answers. As with providing directions from here to there, there are so many routes to take—to speed along the highway, to wander back roads, to forsake the car entirely and hike into the woods and over the ridge. What's more, these are the very questions our students are drawn to during class discussions, the ones they argue the longest and loudest; these are the ideas we debate with our colleagues in the hallways and at the corner bar.

These unanswered questions have led us to reflect upon creative nonfiction, to reflect on the far, dark edges of our genre that the textbooks seldom write about. These questions have led us to think about the historical and contemporary borderlands between fiction and nonfiction, about the illusion of time on the page, about the mythology of memory, about poetry and process and the use of received forms, about the impact of technology on our writerly lives, about immersive research and the power of witness, about achronology and collage, about what we write and why we write. About truth, about the telling of true stories, our stories.

To help us think through these ideas and issues, we contacted a number of writers we admire, writers exploring different territories throughout the realm of creative nonfiction, and asked them to write toward a question they have regarding our genre. The responses were overwhelming. So many writers were already thinking and writing about these very same issues. So many writers wanted to build upon this conversation. So many writers knew that there was so much more we needed to discuss concerning our fourth genre. In the end we chose for inclusion here eighteen of the strongest, most vital craft essays submitted, essays by writers who are Pulitzer Prize–, National Book Award–, and National Book Critic Circle Award–finalists; writers whose work has appeared in *Harper's Magazine, The New York Times Magazine, The Georgia Review, The Missouri Review, The Believer, The Sun, Orion, Creative Nonfiction, Fourth Genre, River Teeth, Brevity*, and numerous volumes of *Best American Essays*; writers who are also scholars, journalists, poets, novelists, book reviewers, and editors; writers whose literary memoirs were pioneers of the form and writers whose edgy essays are now breaking all the rules— we chose for inclusion in this craft anthology eighteen fascinating and essential essays by writers intimately involved with the issues facing creative nonfiction.

Yet—and please read this as both caution and enticement—there are no definitive answers here. This collection aspires only to further the conversation you might already be having with friends, colleagues, students, and mentors. We hope the essays in this anthology deepen and complicate those conversations and push against your various definitions of, boundaries around, and reasons for writing creative nonfiction. We hope these essays provide you new ways of thinking about and making essays and memoirs. We hope the essays in this anthology challenge us all as creative nonfiction writers to travel deeper into those underexplored territories.

Each essay collected here deals intimately with the process of creative non-fiction writing and, often, is a model of the very writing it seeks to inspire. Yet rather than merely offering lists of how-tos or things to try at home, rather than serving as a textbook, this collection of craft essays asks readers to envision creative nonfiction as a living, breathing, raging form of writing. *The Far Edges of the Fourth Genre: Explorations in Creative Nonfiction* assumes readers are familiar with the foundations of the genre and so straightaway wonders at the bats in the attic, the leaks in the half-finished basement, that strange pegboard bathroom door.

And understanding creative nonfiction as an alive and evolving form of writing demands that we understand the more recent historical roots of the genre, especially as we know it in the academy today. So we begin this anthology with a prologue, a look back to how one influential writer of creative nonfiction entered the conversation. Mary Clearman Blew's essay, "Walking Home," deals with the accidental nature of Blew's immersion into creative nonfiction. Blew, in her early career as a teacher and writer of fiction, takes a new university job, which asks her to teach a class in the budding and mostly unexplored genre of creative nonfiction. In this creative non-fiction classroom in the late 1980s, despite her newness to the genre, Blew finds herself drawn to this genre she knows so little about but immediately understands as deeply important, even necessary, in her students' lives—as well as her own. "Walking Home" carries the reader of this anthology along on a journey of one teacher entering the modern creative nonfiction classroom.

With that essay serving as our border crossing and entry, the rest of the book allows each of the authors space to make their arguments about creative nonfiction and express their joys, worries, and curiosities as writers of true stories. Ander Monson compares the essay to the phone hacking he did as a young man. Brenda Miller explores how the Internet affects our experiences and representations of the real. Later, Nancer Ballard examines how time is constructed to understand how time might work within the true story. Both Kim Barnes and Dinty Moore, in very different ways, question how to understand why we are writing and what our stories mean. Erik Reese ends the anthology as he writes about why creative nonfiction might need to be more overtly political.

And we hope that as you wander your way through this book (whether from front to back or by skipping around the book, searching for your own thematic connections) you too begin to ask your own questions about creative nonfiction, about writing, about your writerly life. We hope the essays here inspire, challenge, and complicate your own essays and memoirs. We hope you find here maps and provender for your own explorations in the far country of creative nonfiction.

WALKING HOME

1960

A winter evening in Missoula, Montana. Snow blows against the blackened window behind Dr. Leslie Fiedler, who sits at the head of a conference table in one of the smaller classrooms in the liberal arts building at the University of Montana. Ten or twelve of us are gathered around the table, listening as Dr. Fiedler reads aloud my short story, "Custis for Us at the U."

My story is about a high school football star who doesn't want to go to college but is being pressured to accept a scholarship. Dr. Fiedler reads very well. He is a thickset bearded man with a mane of dark hair and pale, penetrating eyes that rise often from the pages to scan our faces. Many of the citizens of western Montana believe he is evil—he is liberal, urban, and Jewish, after all—but I'm only nineteen and I don't understand why it's evil to be liberal or what it means when he's attacked in letters to the student newspaper for being an existentialist. I live for his word of praise.

I have taken previous creative writing classes (I have never heard them called workshops) from several professors here at the university. The famous Walter Van Tilburg Clark had left Missoula for Reno, Nevada, before I ever arrived, but he left his mark on the English department, and we creative writing students have been assigned "The Portable Phonograph" and "Indian Well" again and again. There was Robert O. Bowen, who had written several novels and taught my freshman honors class but left Montana in some kind of huff, and there was buff, elderly Henry V. Larom, who had written a series of young adult mysteries known as the Mountain Pony books. Dr. Seymour Betsky taught the evening creative writing class at least once, and so did a youngish man I remember only because he remarked that Katherine Anne Porter's story "The Grave" wasn't much good, being about birth and such, of interest only to women.

Now, however, the evening creative writing classes seem to belong to Dr. Fiedler. Many years later I will suspect the various waves and shifts over creative writing were symptoms of something seismic in that English department. It was an English department, after all, and an English department that, in a few years, would hire a poet named Richard Hugo and inaugurate a then-unheard-of MFA degree in creative writing. But in 1960 I am unsuspicious and uninformed and interested only in Dr. Fiedler's opinion of my short story.

That he's reading my work aloud is a sign of the times. We have a copy center on campus where we can leave off typescript to be duplicated and picked up the next day, but the usual procedure in the creative writing classes is for the students to give their stories to the instructor, who selects the pieces he wants to read aloud during the weekly class meeting. We are expected to listen and comment on each other's work, based on what we've just heard and can recall. Previous instructors have given us a few rules for writing fiction. (Dr. Fiedler isn't much for laying down rules for writing.) The first line of a story, we've been taught, should state the theme of the story as a whole, although not in so many words. A story's conclusion should contain a moment of revelation; if it doesn't, it's not a story but a sketch. Also, a story's viewpoint should never shift. We all listen vigilantly for shifting points of view in each other's work.

My story ends with my football star, finding no way out of his dilemma, running through the streets of his hometown with no goal in sight. Dr. Fiedler reads the final sentence and lays the typed pages on the table in front of him. Looks around the table and waits.

Most of the students who look back at him are young men, who may reflect the campus ratio of men to women more than they indicate a male interest in writing. These men have read Hemingway and understand that stories should be about violent death or life in the military, or they've read Kerouac and understand that stories should be about gifted artists who have no money but travel a lot, smoke a lot, and drink a lot of wine. Another sign of our times is that there's no explicit sex and few obscenities in theirs or any other stories, although there are plenty of thwarted relationships followed by despair.

"I just thought it was a boring story," says the large young man sitting next to Dr. Fiedler. "I couldn't get interested in—what was his name?"

A sophomore, daughter of a well-known Montana writer, suggests that the minor characters in the story are stereotypes.

"I just feel like I've read it before, somewhere," says another student, raising her eyebrows and sighing, as though to imply that the story, with its boring stereotypical characters, has been plagiarized.

"Did the point of view shift? I can't remember," says somebody else.

Other opinions rise around the table, few favorable. We tend not to like each other's work, although there are a few alliances and separate conversations among students who have shared previous classes, like my friend Marcy Melton, who like me is married and lives off campus. Marcy writes wonderful stories about long silences between husbands and wives, which I listen to with bitter envy. But tonight I wait through the discussion for the only opinion that matters. Finally Dr. Fiedler picks up the sheets of my story and shuffles them into a stack. "The interesting thing," he says, "is that, in the end, the main character falls back on the one thing he's good at, which is running."

Is this praise? I can't be certain; it's impossible to be certain what Dr. Fiedler is thinking, or what he perceives when he scans our faces with those pale eyes. I'm terrified of him, of course. I can hardly bring myself to speak in his presence. But—the interesting thing—at least he's not condemning my story; at least he's read it, and he's found something worthy of comment in it. If this is not praise, at least it's enough for me to live on and write until time for class next week.

1988

An early spring evening in Lewiston, Idaho, where I came to live last fall and teach at Lewis-Clark State College. The town of Lewiston stretches itself along the confluence of the Clearwater and Snake rivers, sheltered by the great gray river bluffs and blessed by a mild climate that allows magnolias and dogwoods to blossom in the shadow of the Rocky Mountains. On campus the pink and white petals float down to the lawns and flowerbeds while water sprinklers swish in the gathering darkness.

LCSC began as the state normal school, to train teachers. In the 1960s, during the throes of a financial crisis in Idaho, the legislature actually closed the college, which stood empty and deteriorating while ivy grew through the windows of Spalding Hall, where the English department offices currently are located. Opening its doors again to students in the 1970s, the college gradually found a new niche for itself, not only in its wide range of vocational and technical programs, but as a doorway for the so-called nontraditional student. In 1988 the average age for a student here is about thirty-three, and all the professors have gotten used to seeing graying, timorous heads among the eighteen-year-olds.

Last Chance State College, its detractors call it, but in the short time I've taught here, I've come to realize that the nickname is accurate, although not in the way it's intended. A last chance, yes, for the divorced woman with children to support, who writes painfully that she knows an education is the only way she'll ever get herself and the kids out of that basement apartment and on their way. A last chance in a different way for the retired man of fixed income who tells me that the college library and the college classrooms offer him the least expensive and most stimulating experience of his life.

A last chance, for that matter, for me.

I've been away from teaching for the past ten years, working as the dean of arts and sciences at a remote state college in northern Montana. Being a dean had turned me into a person I didn't really like. Academic administration has its own arcane language of hints and codes and what is known in the diplomatic world as double tracking; that is, saying one thing and doing another. Language—words—mattered to me. But in the ten years I was a dean, I did not write a word of fiction worth keeping.

Now, at Lewis-Clark State College, I'm back in the classroom again, feeling as though I'm starting over as a teacher and a writer. I learned to teach freshman composition by trial and error years ago, under the benevolent rule of Willoughby Johnson at the University of Missouri, and I'm fine with my freshman writing classes and also with my survey of British literature and my Shakespeare class I've been assigned. But this evening I'm meeting a class in the writing of creative nonfiction, and it's a new venture for me as well as for the eighteen students who have arranged themselves in a loose circle, waiting to begin. My only guide to teaching creative writing, let alone this new genre of creative nonfiction that seems to have sprung up overnight, is what I can remember from Dr. Fiedler's long-ago evening classes. Should I read somebody's work aloud and see what the students say about it?

About half of the students in our circle are what we've come to call "traditional." That is, they started college right out of high school and now, as juniors or seniors, are in their late teens or early twenties. Two or three others are local schoolteachers, perhaps picking up recertification credits. But a sizeable group can charitably be called "older," if not downright elderly. Most are women, with one or two men, all white haired and favoring the forgiving shapelessness of polyester slacks and sweatshirts. What they hope, as I have discovered, is to rescue their childhoods.

So I now search through my stack of craft books on writing, sent to me by publishers who hope I will require my students to buy them. I've found plenty of advice at the self-help level for writing poetry or fiction or even drama, but hardly anything on this new genre that is getting plenty of fun poked at it—defined by what it is not, etc.—but little that will help the traditional students get started, or the schoolteachers get grades of A, or the older folks relive the past. So I've borrowed and patched pieces of advice where I can, and one of my borrowings tells students to note on each other's work anything they don't understand.

Tonight we're discussing a draft written by a student who probably is in her seventies. She has told us that she spent her childhood in a lumber camp near Pierce, Idaho, a place with no resonance for me, but whose mention makes all the older students smile and shake their heads. Unlike me and my snotty little fellow students at the University of Montana, these people tend to love each other's work.

"We used to get real snow in Pierce, snow like you never see nowadays! The snow would get so deep that the path my father shoveled from the kitchen door to the outhouse would eventually get to be a tunnel, and we would be glad of that tunnel all winter long," she has written.

Her friends nod their heads in corroboration of the snow depth of years past, and one or two raise their hands and contribute anecdotes of their own.

The writer continues. "My mother would wash our clothes and hang them outside to freeze-dry on the line. Then she would bring them inside, sprinkle them, and iron them."

There's a pause. A twenty-year-old studies his copy of her draft (we've progressed at least to the point of having copies of each other's work for everyone to read ahead of time). He raises his hand. "You told us to mark anything we didn't understand. What exactly did her mother do to the clothes? *Sprinkle?* What's that?"

In the silence, as the old folks exchange startled looks, I have a flash of all the time that has passed for them and also for me. How can I ever tell the story of my own life, even to my own children?

The next morning, in Spalding Hall, I join the little group standing around the main office and tell the story of the young man who didn't know what it meant to sprinkle clothes. The department secretary laughs.

"I grew up in Illinois," she says, "and the weather in summer was so humid that the sprinkled clothes would mildew overnight, so my mother would roll them in towels and put them in the refrigerator. We all got used to seeing those long ropy rolls of laundry whenever we went for a soda."

"My mother would put a perforated cap on a pop bottle and fill it with water to sprinkle the clothes," says somebody else.

Hearing their stories, I don't feel quite as antiquated as I did last night. And through the witchcraft of association, I'm seeing the flash of my mother's hand, dipped in water (she wouldn't have bothered with filling a pop bottle and shaking it) to dash over her dry clothes before she bundles them into a bath towel. Then the odor of burning wood, flatirons heating on the stove, and a shape, like a mist rising over the ironing board from the starch and the steam, or a materialization of this strange genre of creative nonfiction.

2010

A few years ago I moved "up the hill," as they say in Lewiston, to help inaugurate the MFA program in creative writing at the University of Idaho. One of the graduate students in the first creative nonfiction class I taught at the university wrote in an evaluation, *I don't think she knows a thing about rhetoric or composition theory.* The student was right. I've tried to read some of the theory, but I grasp it only by translating it into story as I go along. My impression—maybe my illusion—is that the rhetoricians live by precepts that guide their writing through a more rigorous and orderly process than my fumbling for images.

Do rhetoricians feel pain? I've often wondered. *I felt a little gross writing about something so painful for my family*, writes one of my current graduate students. *Plumbing for my parents' reaction, running to my room to copy snatches of dialogue. What an asshole I am. Is that what nonfiction writers are made to do?*

All I can tell her is how I feel when I write about a dead husband, or about a still-living ex-husband whose follies, forty years ago, were no worse than my own.

Our MFA program is strong and competitive, and we've managed to maintain its integrity even as higher education in Idaho is battered by our current financial crisis (how many more, Lord, how many more). Our students submit their work for publication, and some of it is accepted, and some of our graduates have gone on to good tenure-track jobs, teaching writing. In workshops these days we look up from our perusal of each other's drafts to discuss the current questions: whether it is important to keep to factual truth in creative nonfiction or whether, as some well-known writers insist, it's more important to present "emotional truth"; whether dialogue can be crafted in nonfiction; whether characters can be conflated; whether a timeline can be condensed. Is a pastiche fraudulent? Can a montage be created on the page? And always, always, students worry about the issues of honesty and betrayal. They worry about the pundits who warn that memoir writing is lazy writing and advise that they ought to be writing fiction, and I wonder why fiction is thought to plumb more "truth" than nonfiction does, when the boundary between the two genres, as I've written elsewhere, is as fluid as water, and when in either genre it's the witchcraft of association and the projection of imagination that opens doorway after doorway in the haunted labyrinth that folds and unfolds and never comes to an end.

So many voices to tell us what we ought not to write.

> To write about other people is a betrayal.
> To write about yourself is naval-gazing.

Discussions of craft are more sophisticated than ever before. We talk about focus and narrative arc. We consider linear and nonlinear structures. When we discuss shifting points of view, it's to decide whether to shift and why. Moments of revelation? The term seems dated.

I'm more fluent than I once was in the terminology of craft, and when I leave a literature class to teach a creative writing class, I don't feel the old awkward panic, as though I'm in one of those dreams where I've agreed to perform in grand opera and find myself on stage, naked, without being able to sing a note.

But when I remember those classes that Dr. Fiedler presided over, I remember those pale eyes scanning us with a hint of withheld amusement. What did he know that we didn't? That whether we're writing fiction or creative nonfiction, and however sophisticated the workshop discussion, what matters is the day-in, day-out work, the writing to meet the deadline, the presentation to the audience. The one or two words of praise to live on for the next week.

The lonely walk home to start rewriting.

ANDER MONSON

ESSAY AS HACK

I fear for the essay, friends, and its bad reputation. It feels white and dull, dusty, old. Encased in tombs like the *Oxford Book of Essays*. Each year's *Best American* is not a yawn, exactly, since some of the individual essays are good enough when read and thought about, but as a whole they are not particularly inviting, exciting, compelling. They lack, what, pizzazz? Flash? Flare? Fireworks? Prestidigitation? Say what you want about the spectacle of memoir, but it at least seems timely. Hot. Fresh. Glittery. Fake. It has the veneer of reality or reality show. It as much as anything else appears to be about the stuff of our lives, or the wished stuff of our lives: suffering, crime, sexual politics, revelation, television, possibly hot tubs, body waxing, celebrity, and bikinis. You know a memoir might be trashy but it will entertain us. But essays? They are easy chairs. Thinky. Stable. The nice sensitive older guy driving a '92 Volvo. The smell of aged pine. They are sedentary. They connote senescence. Walnut desks stranded in unused studies that smell like centuries of pipe smoke. You have to admit it does not feel like a youthful form.

All of this sob story for the essay is concurrent with the declining technology of the newspaper, the literary journal, and other print media that gave rise to many of the essay's brightest stars. We still have commentary but it's moved online. It's become increasingly an amateur sport. Distributed via blog and Amazon reviews by Top 500 Reviewers to you, the consumer. Perhaps it's only fair.

Maybe the lyric essay is an exception. A sparkler, a firecracker on a summer evening. It alone is saucy, upper lip curled. Flirty in its assignations with poetry. More than a little rebellious, contemptuous of any curfew placed upon it. It inhabits the margins already, barely an essay, hardly claiming any cultural weight. We'll return to this lonely roamer later.

A sigh: a sigh was my response to the essay when I discovered it. I did not lack love for its meanderings, its attempts to convey the motions of thought, but it felt remote. Isolated. Writ in stone and handed down. Unapproachable. The production of years of pristine thinking and immersion journalism. It is seemingly inaccessible from an artist's standpoint without deploying some kind of wizardry.

As an enthusiast of literary forms, I faced the wall. I looked up it, looked around it. Saw only wall and wall and wall. Brick after brick. No chink. No crinkle in its face.

This is one trajectory.

Introduction to the Hack

Hacking is at heart a creative activity. It is first, simply, an exploration, an opening up, of a system. A kind of problem solving. When we say *hack*, we probably mean to illegally access a computer system by any one of various means, probably by someone geeky, eggheaded, to plant a virus in some high-level Department of Defense computer, but that's reductive, pejorative, sloppy thinking. Most hackers who illegally access computer (or other) systems do it not to break the law but because we want access. Because we see a system and we are not allowed inside it. Because we see that apparently impenetrable tower and we want to know what rests within its walls.

More loosely, a hack is an ingenious use of technology to accomplish something that is otherwise impossible to accomplish. It is a bridge from one land mass to another over deep water. It appears, like any sufficiently advanced technology, as a kind of magic. It comes out of the insoluble. It is surprising. Pleasing. Amazing.

For instance, a famous hardware hack, the red box, repurposes a Radio Shack autodialer (a portable, pre-cell-phone device that could store and automatically dial numbers) via some soldering to mimic the tone (technically a series of four tones) that indicates to a pay phone that a quarter has been deposited, allowing me to call anywhere for free. The blue box (the even more famous hardware hack) generated the 2600 Hz tone and allowed a hacker (well, technically the term is *phone phreak*) to take control of the trunk line and go wherever he wanted to go in the phone system. These hardware hacks commanded knowledge of a system (often discovered accidentally, or through long evenings of trial and error) to accomplish control.

For some users of the red box, the device is about free calls. For others it is about the act of accessing the network, of bypassing a lock quite ingeniously; it allows further exploration, node by node, of a network.

But regardless the hack is the trick, not what use it's put to.

I have lived the life of accessing networks, exploring PBX systems and phone lines, been publicly punished for it, for my audacity. For gaining illegal access to credit cards, to databases of hundreds of thousands of credit cards. I didn't use the credit cards for anything: I simply wanted access to them, to the growing, private world of information stored on thousands of servers lined up, hidden away in banks of modems. Because I could, I tell myself, I wanted in.

I hesitate to try to ascribe a particular motivation to my actions in retrospect. The brain reconfigures memory, reorders events, resets them among other events to form narrative, causality: it creates sense. The mind tells itself stories about what happens to it. So me saying that I did X because of Y rests on thousands of assumptions about who or what I think I am, how I thought of myself then—transmuted into how I think about myself now. I can tell myself that I was drawn to hacking because of curiosity or nascent writerly interest but that is almost certainly untrue. Who knows why I did what I did, why I broke into Michigan Bell trucks armed with smoke bombs and center punches and mace in case the cops arrived? And who knows what I would have done with the mace if the cops arrived? Any sort of attempt to sort meaning from the past is fraught in thousands on thousands of ways, exponentially splintering. The more you think about it the more it asymptotically approaches impossibility.

This is not to suggest we shouldn't attempt it. The attempt is glorious, and attempting rewires the brain. It moves the circuitry around, attaching a new conclusion to an action, reconstructing self. In a way, thinking about the self hacks it.

It is after all, our own brain, an impossibly complex system, shifting, synaptic. It is *the* system, the main subject for literature of any sort, the perfect subject, also seemingly inaccessible.

The memoir appears to try to understand but mostly it narrates. Airs action out, reveals it. It offers us confession, prepackaged narrative arc: redemption, for instance. It thinks it thinks but it does not quite get there.

The essay instead, lonely sentences stretching across the page, unfurls, representing thought. The essay affords us the best way to hack this system.

Essay as Game

Let me take another shot at it.

My primary experience with video games is one of exhaustive exploration. While I can't quite admit the level of exhaustive play that characterizes those who write completist walkthroughs for, say, *Final Fantasy XII*, which I have logged 110 hours playing on the PS2 (helpfully the game tracks my addictive hours), I do spend a lot of time thinking about and being immersed in game worlds.

"Split Infinity," the writer who compiled the FAQ/Walkthrough I have been consulting for some of the more arcane secrets that the game holds, is one of these super-exhaustive players slash writers. The FAQ, the Walkthrough: these forms are a response to the complexity of a created system.

The FFXII FAQ is exceptionally exhaustive (a sort of split infinity). It is 1,600 pages. 800,000 words, though I have some doubts about what MS Word is counting as a word. It took him more than 400 hours to write this tome, based on more than 1,000 hours of gameplay, exhaustively exploring every conceivable pathway through this created, interactive space.

I would argue this is essay, even as it is an informative document. It is a record of an individual (and eventually collaborative) exploration of a system. It is a fairly ingenious solution to a problem: where can gamers go to find information about how to get the Zodiac Spear, for instance (the answer is *very* far from obvious). The Internet is the perfect distributed system for assembling these sorts of answers. For hacking the problem into soluble chunks and distributing it across thousands of players' experiences. Split Infinity has done it for us. It is a staggering achievement.

Too, it is a hack. Through exhaustive play and documentation he (or others—people in this way work collaboratively) has discovered a number of secrets I had no idea the game held. He has accessed secret rooms in the dungeon, and he's given us the key. He's opened up hidden areas in the system. His FAQ lists sixty-one easily missable things in the game.

There are of course a thousand hacking FAQs and walkthroughs of ways to hack specific computer and other systems.

Reading these FAQs—or, better, writing them—adds pathways to the brain. Adds syntax where there was none. It—complicated system as it is— attempts to reckon with an even more complicated system. To map it out. To render it inert, paused, interrupted, in another form.

Essay as Simulated Mind

The essay tries hard to solidify the motions of thought. It—more than most other forms of writing—is not as beholden to tradition, restriction. Sure, it's, like, old. Totally AARP. We can date it back to Montaigne, or, trying harder, Seneca. I have to admit that Montaigne bores me. Seneca, too, really, and most of what we call the moral essayists, publicly thinking about individual behavior as part of a society, offering suggestions for better living, and so on. Maybe it's my age. Maybe it's that I want to sex it up.

The essay does not rely on narrative arc (though it can). It does not rely on lyric motion (though it can). It can potentially incorporate anything, draw from anything, in search of the range of motion of human thought that it attempts to present.

It is a sticky ball. It is the video game *Katamari Damacy*. It accommodates. Like the brain.

Each essay we read is as close as we can get to another mind. It is a simulation of the mind working its way through a problem. This is not to suggest that every essay is good, revelatory, successful, fruitful, interesting. But stepping into an essay is stepping into the writer's mind. We are thrown into the labyrinth, a huge stone rolling behind us. It is a straight shot of the brain in all its immediacy, its variety, strands of half-remembered text, partly-thought-through ideas, images below the surface of memory. We are thrown into *process:* of thinking, which is like an algorithm, a machine for replicating or simulating thought:

So, a quote from Theodor Adorno's essay "The Essay as Form" to add to our ball, a line to add to our algorithm, one strand of thinking: "The essay is decried as a hybrid; that it is lacking a convincing tradition; that its strenuous requirements have only rarely been met: all this has been often remarked upon and censured."

Here we find ourselves. We find ourselves plucked out of our lives and are transplanted in the middle of a mind. A plot, really, strung together of thought. Of a linguistic situation. An argument. Given that the essay lacks tradition, what then? And later: "Luck and play are essential to the essay. It does not begin with Adam and Eve but with what it wants to discuss; it says what is at issue and stops where it feels itself complete—not where nothing is left to say."

Adorno tries to describe what the essay does. It thinks. It plays. It discusses. It cuffs at ideas as if they were a ball. It is discursive. It cures nothing. It might occasionally curse. Naturally it is subjective, but it owns that subjectivity and strives to comprehend and transcend it. It has its stated subject (in Adorno's case, trying to work out the form of the essay in the historical situation he finds it in), but all essays' implied subjects are the essay itself, the mind of the writer, the I in the process of sifting and perceiving, even if the I is itself only implied, never apparent, hidden underneath the shroud of formal argument. *Who argues*, we ask. A pause. Silence. Awkward moment. Then: *I do*, it responds weakly.

The essay claims its own limits and works within them: as it works, so does the mind. As the argument shifts, cuts back, or redoubles, uncovering something the essay did not know it knew (for that is every essay's purpose, to wend, explore, to sidetrack as it must), so go the processes of the mind. It freezes thought for us. Of course this fixity is a lie: one line of thought extends and becomes yesterday, diaspora. The second time through an essay in revision we are not the same combination of brain and body; the network has shifted and what we thought we thought is no longer what we think. And by thinking we erase or redouble thought, confirming or denying it. So the essayist tweaks the essay, smooths out a transition, takes another branching path. And that version of thought is fixed and left, a pathway in the brain, graphite trace on the page. And on and on until the essayist gets up and gives it up. The essay should change on every public reading or recitation as something new occurs. But it's impossible in art. Finally we have to let it go and hope it will show the reader something new.

Reading essays gets us closer to others' thinking, or at least the most recent version. Writing them gets us closer to our own. It at least allows us to interrupt the constant motion of our minds to put something down and consider it, think about it from a year removed, or from space on the shuttle, or in a different space, overlooking another view from a new hotel in a different city.

And what about the lyric essay? Have we forgotten it? It proceeds in chunks, disconnected fragments. It pauses, tacks around the subject, or dead-ends through white space.

In some ways the lyric essay is the most essay sort of essay.

Our lyric variety of the essay is a polyglot. It is pansexual. If the essay is a ball, the lyric essay is a super sticky power ball. But calling the essay lyric doesn't add all that much. It specifies, I guess, that this essay is a lyric one. It closes down some of the dimensions through which the essay might move.

Essay itself is already polymorphic. It is oversexed in its potential union with anything: polemic, story, treatise, argument, fact, fiction, lyric.

But lyric has freshened up the essay world, it seems, so we should be grateful.

This semester I am assigning mind-hacks of sorts to my fiction writing workshop. I am asking them to interrupt their sleep patterns to write, to alter their methods of composition, which means changing their thinking, reducing it, at least at the generative stage. To feel the force necessary to strike keys on a manual typewriter. To only write in abandoned buildings. To dictate into a microphone. To write hungry. Exhausted. If I could, I'd prescribe some psychotropic drugs. The brain gets used to its own strategies when we write. It finds the path of least resistance, like a liquid on a surface. It moves. It settles into ruts. I am trying to get my students to write from different mental states, to find their way to different voices. I think of this as a way of hacking the brain, to get it—technology as it is—to go someplace it is unaccustomed to. I want them to try to feed it different stories, different stimuli, in an attempt to get it to generate different sorts of texts.

Essay as Interruption

The world moves. Art stops it. The essay stops it. It is a temporary thing, but necessary. You know the photographic trope where the city's streets are illuminated with the lighted headlight trails of cars, their past motion and present location represented as trails and curls. Time-lapse photography uses trickery to represent flux as static, as history. Beauty occurs in isolation, from a distance. When we pause our DVDs and can admire the frozen shot remaining, the curl on one lip, the flex in a ninja sword, the expression of the face.

The essay, like a poem, acts as fermata. It processes ideas, images, texts, or objects at its own speed. It rewinds, meditates, circles, returns, sits and spins if it must. And it should. It is, like all good art, an interruption, an intervention between the world and the mind. Its status as a weird sort of hybrid comes from this. Stories have forward motion. They are driven by what happens. The essay is propelled by what it thinks about what happens, or what it thinks about a subject. It turns the subject in its mind. It gets all self-conscious. Too self-conscious sometimes. The essay can lock up, find its way to infinite recursion: what do I think about what I think about what I think about etc.? If left undisturbed, thinking can spiral down.

The essay-space is a dreaming space. Everything is allowed. It might move erratically, as in dreams, with its own logic. It can tangent out, follow a line as far as it can go.

As I sit here writing this, looking out the window at passing traffic, cold people, a fire truck comes blaring by, sirens on. An ambulance follows. My gaze here—my train of thought, too—is interrupted. Back to regularly scheduled traffic programming. Two minutes later another fire truck blows by, moving fast. These vehicles are en route to intervention. A home might be on fire. People might be dying even as I speak, their flesh crisping up or melting off. It could be a false alarm. If I were a real investigative essayist, or journalist, I'd be up and in my car, on their trail, trying to dodge the resuming traffic, hoping to see something exciting or terrible.

I am not. I haven't moved. A girl opens the door across the street. The pizza delivery guy is inside. Nothing is happening. They are both just sitting there. Her boyfriend, apparently wearing Zubaz, looking a little like an animal, shows up from the back. There is a transaction. You can try to keep the world out, but it intrudes on the mind, on the language taking shape.

I believe in interruptions. I believe in sidetracks. The pizza guy is from Domino's. I used to deliver Domino's in Ames, Iowa. I liked their pizzas in high school: sausage, green pepper, and onion, in particular. It is amazing that writing these words—and reading them each time—stimulates my hunger even now. Take that, brain! Take that, body!

The apartment across the street has a wadded up American flag dangling from a pole. This must mean something but I know not what. Perhaps if I think about it long enough, allow the mind—and the sentence—to swirl around it, it will dream and yield up its meaning (or I can fool myself into thinking that it will yield its meaning).

Essay accommodates. It expands. It contracts. It is a flexible technology.

The good essay advantages itself of interruption. Thinking, after all, is not dramatic. Because it is isolated, potentially pure mind, it can spin and spin. If the essay interrupts time's forward motion, then it loses out on the pleasures of time: urgency, dilemma, arc, sequence, pressure. Left without constraint, the essay languishes. Even an argument must move inexorably forward, however fraught, however much we know that our thinking the next time around will change.

Of course any text moves forward. It reads (and composes) word by word, sequentially, line by line and on down the page. It stacks up like in Tetris. It creates pressure on the thinking. Even as the essay diverges in its thought processes, as it follows tangents and diversions, there's still the expectation of convergence, of a final arc. We want the essay to rise and take its shape. We want to be pleased. We want cohesion. Maybe we want redemption for your or our sins. We want rising and falling action, even in essay. The smart essayist knows this. She uses the reader's expectations to her advantage. She understands that even faced with infinity we need constraint.

I believe in the fragment. It's the most honest representation of anything. It acknowledges gaps, its lack of comprehensiveness, its ability to surround and control a subject, an idea.

Of the literary forms, the essay is the most open to fragment. Because it tries to represent thinking, it knows only so much. It constantly faces the edge of what it knows and stares off the edge into a darkness filled with question marks. The essay is *about* limitations. It understands itself. Because it forgoes much of the structure of poem or story, it gets by on its own ability to expand and consume whatever we feed it. It is self-replicating, expanding like a virus.

Perhaps it's more accurate to say an essay is like a worm, spreading across systems, sending out new shoots. It is modular, nodular.

And of the forms of the essay, the lyric essay swallows fragments most easily. In order to accommodate gap, the essay must ape the poem—it must create an openness, an attention to beauty rather than meaning, at least on the micro-scale, it must jump through gaps and continue on, an elision of the white space on the page.

I am a writer who likes constraint. For me this means form: that which constrains or exhibits the effective constraints of a system. It is an obsession. Forms come in dreams. They structure dreams. They embody system. The outline is a system. The index is a system, or it relies on system. Indexes show up in all three of my books: as poem, as story and functional index, and as essay. So the essay begins for me with the acknowledgment of system. This limits the motion, the options for the essayist. It allows the thinking and rhetoric to expand and run along the edge. This is what hacking does. Hacking engages with a system, with its physical or digital limitations, the impossibility of access to parts of the system, for instance, without authorization. The limits of the Unix structure of read/write/alter rights. The limits of human ingenuity when it comes to choosing passwords (hint: we are not very ingenious at all).

A form is like a challenge. A wall. A system of rules. A dungeon. Signifiers accessing other signifiers. Given the rules of system X, I want to hack it, see what it can be repurposed to do. In this way writing the essay accesses the system, breaks the locks off of it, pushes against it, line by line, and *transforms*.

My friend Nicole has a purse made out of candy wrappers woven together. It is a beautiful object: glossy, slick, enclosing, crafty. I find myself wanting to fill it with candy but in practice she fills it with the usual stuff of a purse, a world I don't typically have much access to. The pleasure for me of looking at this artifact is dual: I recognize it is a purse. On closer inspection we see it is made up of candy wrappers. It is both things and neither, and in so doing it is something more. It is transformed.

It is also falling apart. It is an object transformed into another object. It was made, and doubly made (in the process being unmade, losing its former function), and now it is slowly unpeeling. I wonder if the half-life of the object is intentional. That, like a candy wrapper, it is finally disposable, reducing to the memory of what it contained, a ruin.

I write this essay on my new word processing program. It's called WriteRoom, and it is fantastic. The screen I am writing on mimics the look (in some ways) of a green-screen monochrome monitor, the kind you'd find on an Apple IIc, for instance, or an old IBM PC. In this way the writing of this—the essaying of it, for I have only a vague sense of where I hope this essay to go—is physically not all that dissimilar from my experience sitting in front of computer screens looking at the login prompt of a BSD Unix system or the entry point for an unknown database, announcing almost nothing about itself. I am there again in one dorm room or another, or downstairs in the basement of my parents' split-level, thinking about ordering Domino's and quaffing Cokes, fingering my bag of dodecahedron D&D dice, playing some Sisters of Mercy on my boom box bought from a duty free shop in Dubai. I am feeling cool. The world is stretched out in front of me, accessible via keyboard, via text input into a machine. It is a series of walls and gateways. This is a generative space for me. It is like a dream. It is light spreading out in darkness (green light growing on the black screen). It is like an electric dungeon.

Hacks surround us. The world is made of them, of ingenuities. Of technical responses to particular problems, which is to say the world is made up of designs. The essay is one of these, a technology repurposed in any given instance to solve a sort of problem, one that it does not know it is meant to solve until it solves it. It is an exploration; it serves the function of art, treading out in darker waters.

Even this essay—especially this essay—is a hack. Given the idea *an essay is a hack* I have been trying to find ways to make it work, to wave my hands, trace my thoughts, produce language, produce magic.

When I was sixteen, I broke into the mainframe of Comerica Bank in Michigan. The details are now distant. It was simple. Really no hack at all. It required a couple minutes of guessing passwords. Once I found the dial-in number it led to an unlocked door. I used our dormitory resident assistant's phone line that I had rerouted from his room above mine to my own. Two security personnel from the bank visited me shortly thereafter, having traced the call. I hadn't thought to try to make my number more difficult to trace; in a way it did not occur to me that they might take offense at my exploration, my intrusion. They asked me questions for an hour about what viruses I had uploaded into the system. I was dumbfounded. They expected—or maybe feared—the worst. What I cared about was simply being inside, typing words and sending them through my modem to their modem to their mainframe system, something larger, more complex, more powerful and godlike and awful and other than my personal computer—and having it respond.

Eventually I was not allowed to have a phone line for obvious reasons. I had acquired master keys for the campus that year, and I went about rerouting two phone lines from the switchboard in the basement: one snaked up to my room. I painted the phone line the color of brick (or perhaps I wish I had—there is no way to tell if this is a fabrication; it feels too ingenious in retrospect, the mind says: you weren't quite that crafty) and bent the lead panes in the dorm room window to accommodate the line. The other line I snaked up to my friend Jason's room. We had hollowed out one of the standard-issue dressers so that the drawer faces were just façade. I had installed a computer in his hollow dresser for my BBS, Datacrime International, to run 24-7 on a modem and the rerouted, dedicated line. I admired that hack, that hiding of the machine in the dresser. It was like a literary symbol, I thought to myself appreciatively. Or perhaps I think so now.

I also rewired the phone system of the dorm so that the pay phone was connected to one of the professor's lines, allowing everyone to call for free. It was an elegant solution to a particular problem: being stuck at boarding school with no money, no phone lines, and no way out except the pay phone. I freed that passage up.

None of this was difficult. I did not evade detection. I wasn't all that smart. Many hackers I knew were more ingenious, more serious, than me, more adept with assembler code or with the errata of shadowed password files in BSD Unix. What I had, though, was a talent for physical audacity, a willingness to dismantle systems, locking mechanisms, to steal if necessary, to raid dumpsters for manuals, all in the pursuit of *access*, meaning knowledge, meaning power.

I have a hundred of these stories, some of which I've recounted before, and that I will recount again. They are a cloud of possibility that resides in the brain part of the body that produces this essay. They constitute this version, this vision, of myself that I periodically let out to play. But with technical ability at writing, and the discovery of the pleasure of plundering received forms, a lot of my interest in the hack moved in a literary direction, towards the intricacy of language systems.

And now the language systems interact with the memory system that recalls the hacker exploits, and behind every essay I write is this hacker persona, this desire for punkrockitude, the trickster impulse.

The History of Literature

The history of literature is the history of experimental literature. Thank God. It is—or it mirrors and prefigures—the history of hacking. Of geographic exploration. Of body modification projects. Of medical innovation. Of Star Trek mythologies or other invention. Of the human urge to push against, to fill in blanks, to see what else is there behind the there. What person wants to accomplish simply what has occurred before? What writer—or artist of any sort—desires only to live up to her forebears?

Experiment interacts and sprouts from literary history. Every poem, every story, every essay must still deliver an emotional or intellectual experience, no matter how unusual the form. It must still offer *arc*. It must emanate from a mind and show some trace. It poses questions and resolves at least a few of them. Experiment is a hack of one or more formal element, trying to do without it, to cross a gap. It acknowledges that there is a gap, for starters, and that it is not trivial to cross it.

But those who decry literature as *experimental* are usually saying something is *only* experimental, that it lacks human dimension, that it is all brain, no body, no heart. That it is an experiment that has not borne fruit. But the experiment is the process, not the product.

The problem is colossal: rendering human experience as text. Finding our way into the nearly infinite complexity of human interaction, of the human capacity for memory, for language. Our job as writers, as essay writers, is to set out (dare we say *essay*) with no clear sense of what the results of the experiment will be, but to try to create something of it that is somehow magical.

The last strand—or maybe fragment—of the essay has yet to fall into place, I think, as I prepare for bed, looking out on the spectacular ripple of lights in the city buildings. After a ridiculous battle with the packaging, I get open one of ten individually wrapped pouches of Vanilla Mint–flavored Benadryl Quick Dissolve Strips. That is a lot of adjectives. One of many recent methods of delivering medications (the caplet, the capsule, the tablet, the tab, the gelcap, the liquid) all offering us options to the pill, I have been looking forward to this, I think, for months. I am a huge fan of the Listerine Pocket Pack breath strip. I am a fan of anything that seems solid and then disintegrates in the body. With the pouch finally open, I lay it on my tongue like an offering. Or maybe I am thinking communion. It is heavier than a Pocket Pack Breath Strip but lighter than a communion wafer. It smells tingly. Minty. I am amazed by its technology. On my tongue it holds its form for a minute, longer than I would expect. I watch my mouth in the mirror as it dissolves. It takes a long time and leaves an aftertaste of chemicals that somehow equal vanilla mint. Even now I can feel it in my mouth and I am pleased. I don't know what this means.

BRENDA MILLER

WRITING INSIDE THE WEB: CREATIVE NONFICTION IN THE AGE OF CONNECTION

Free Box

The Free Box always stood on the front porch of the lodge, its heavy lid growing soft at the edges from so many hands lifting and peering in. A Free Box lures you, no matter what else you might be doing at the time. A Free Box is a promise. A Free Box is not a box that is free (though sometimes I did want to cart away the box itself, to have this treasure chest hidden away in my cottage); it's the contents inside that are ready to be given away.

The Free Box I'm remembering lived at Orr Hot Springs in northern California, in the early 80s—an era that believed the universe provided gifts if one knew the right way to ask. The lodge hunkered down in the center of the community, filled with ratty couches and heavy wood dining tables; from the front porch you could watch naked people ambling their way toward the baths. You could watch the herb garden flowering or eavesdrop on romances that kindled and faded on the front lawn. You could watch the light shift over the cliffs that loomed above, and spot red-tailed hawks circling in the updrafts. You could hear pots and pans clanking in the kitchen as people made their communal meals, hair still damp from the sauna. Over it all: the hiss of sulfur from underground, the smell of mineralized steam.[1]

---

1. Here's where, if I turned my wireless connection on, I would probably start moseying around websites looking for information about hot springs, the composition of minerals, etc. But I've turned off the Internet in order to concentrate. Because I know that bit of research would lead me to the shopping sites where I need to buy some stuff for my new hot tub in the backyard. And I need to call the guy about the bamboo hedge, and maybe I should get some fertilizer for the bamboo I already have. Etc. Etc.

You never knew what you might find in the Free Box—usually tattered concert T-shirts, but sometimes there might be something unusually lovely that caught your eye: a tie-dyed scarf, a crocheted shawl, a porcelain teacup with a chipped handle. We never saw anyone actually put anything *in* the Free Box, yet it always seemed full. We did often see people standing in that posture peculiar to someone foraging for the unexpected: one hand holding the lid up, the other sifting through the items as if panning for gold—head bent, eyes intent: the forager wanted to appear disinterested, casual, but the studious tilt of the head gave away the seriousness of this search.

There might be a pair of rainbow suspenders, or a half-empty bottle of olive oil. There might be Birkenstocks worn down at the heel. There might be a long dress with lace at the hem, or a book of swollen, waterlogged poems by Kahlil Gibran, his words now smudged, but still earnest: *To you the earth yields her fruit, and you shall not want if you but know how to fill your hands. It is in exchanging the gifts of the earth that you shall find abundance and be satisfied.*[2]

These were castoffs, yes, but at the time did not feel like castoffs to us, but gifts simply waiting for a home. Or not gifts, exactly, but artifacts of other lives, looking to tell a story. Or not a story, exactly, but a fragment of the web that connects one human being to the next.

When we put on those suspenders, or slipped our bare feet into someone else's grody shoes, we took on a bit of their story, or were free to imagine them: the Wavy Gravy concert in Sonoma, perhaps, and those suspenders walking through a crowd, crisp and bright holding up a pair of baggy pants because belts are just too mainstream, too constricting, *man*. The concert's over and the suspenders now splay in the box, untethered from history, until you pick them up, finger them, put them to work again.

---

2. Okay, so yes, you caught me: I had no Kahlil Gibran memorized, so I clicked on the wireless for *just a minute* to look it up, and lo, it was good: within thirty seconds I had lines from a poem that so perfectly connect to the theme this essay is developing it brings tears to my eyes. Now I can smugly let those lines stand like sentinels at the end of the paragraph, waving their beacons. And now that I have those lines, the essay has moved from embryo to fetus stage, and I understand where I'm going. Now I can get up, make another cup of coffee, look outside at the rain, think about taking a soak in the hot tub, then sit back down again. I'll think about looking at my email since the wireless is back on. And I do. And I send some e-mails. Okay, now I'm back.

Big Ideas

The first time I went on a writing retreat, I had no idea what I was doing. And I went for two months! I arrived at Hedgebrook on Whidbey Island, in the winter of '94, with my clunky Mac Classic in tow, a box of books, a sack full of travel journals, and lots of big ideas about writing.

I soon found out, rather painfully, that Big Ideas about writing often lead you nowhere. Those Big Ideas sit in the middle of the room, daring you to write something good. Something good and something *long.* They glower at you. They grumble and complain. They make you hungry just an hour after breakfast. They give you a whopping headache. They make you look at the clock and wonder if anyone would notice if you just headed home, say, seven weeks early.

The cottage had a padded window seat, a sleeping loft, a tiny woodstove, and a long desk by a window that looked into the woods. The cooks brought your lunch to you in a basket and tiptoed away. You could bicycle to Useless Bay, take long walks there accompanied by sandpipers. You could lose yourself at Useless Bay, and find yourself, and wander every which way in between. You could feel what it was like to be perfectly useless.

The pure beauty and generosity of the place made you extremely grateful and, if you're a neurotic like me, extremely guilty. What had I done to deserve such beneficence?

Though I spent much of my time at Hedgebrook fighting off my own demons, I did write my first long braided essay there: "Basha Leah," an essay that is wholly dependent on the space that grew in me during that time. It's a fragmented piece that told me, gently, that I had to give up my Big Ideas and pay attention to small details instead. It told me to sit still, to wait. It demanded that I simply be quiet.

Back then you really had to dive into yourself on a writing retreat. There were very few distractions—no e-mail, no Internet, only a pay phone in the woodshed. You didn't get much mail because you wouldn't be there for long. You had yourself, and your other self, and maybe another self for company during the day (a tiresome group at best . . .) so you looked forward with inordinate glee to conversation with other writers at the farm table at dinner. Sometimes you wandered into the kitchen early, asked if you could chop a carrot or two, just so you could feel productive at something.

If the cooks felt sympathetic that day, they'd let you. But sometimes they stuck doggedly to the rules of the place: that Hedgebrook is a retreat from everything usually demanded of women. They wouldn't even let us clear our own dishes from the table, so to chop a carrot might be sacrilege. Everything was designed to keep you in the Free Box state of mind: one where the world offers itself to you freely.

So I wandered into the library, picked up a book at random: a book that began speaking to me about my hidden Jewish heritage. Then I went back to my cottage and caught a glimpse of myself in the reflection of a window as I did Tree Pose in the living room. Later, I flipped open my notebook to a page I'd written and forgotten: about a visit to a Portuguese monastery where women pray to Mary's breast.

In the quiet I sat down to write, to weave these random things together and make use of them. To recycle. Reclaim. Such work takes time. Such work requires concentration, sniffing out the trail, crouching, examining scat for signs.

Writing Brain

Now, years later, my Writing Brain could never crouch and wait. It's too nervous; it can barely peep out a few words. My Writing Brain has a kink in its neck and a sore back, it says *Just let me go back to sleep*, then rouses with a groan, a recalcitrant teenager who stayed out past curfew last night, roaming the Internet for a fix—so jumpy, as if on amphetamines, tentacles reaching outward, sticking on voices that aren't really voices (they're all an illusion), and so they exhaust this poor little brain that now just wants to sleep past noon. So you let it sleep upstairs—better a sleeping brain than a cranky brain.

The Writing Brain slumbers hard, drools on the pillow, but you'll shake it awake eventually and force it to come downstairs for breakfast. This brain will grumble and demand coffee and French toast. This brain will linger too long at the table, reading the paper, and when you ask it politely to get dressed, it will snap at you, *Okay, okay*, and then slump into its writing clothes, heave itself into a chair, and stare blankly at the screen a while, until it whines that it needs to check Facebook and e-mail, just in case something important has happened in the last five minutes[3]—and you'll have to be firm, set some boundaries as you have to do with all children.

You'll need to give it positive reinforcement—*See, look what a good sentence you wrote, good job!*—give it the illusion of choice—*You can either write upstairs or on the front porch, those are your choices*—and at some point you'll just have to leave the writing brain to its own devices, trust it, give it some responsibility while you watch discretely from the kitchen.

And you want to tell this brain that *freedom's just another word for nothing left to lose,* and *you don't know what you've got till it's gone.* You want to tell it to find a nice box—but not too nice—and paint it inside and out, then put inside everything that catches its eye: let the box determine how far you can go today; let the box lure you into arrangement.[4] You give your writing brain some supplies, offer what you have.

Here, you say. *Here's a free box.* But your Writing Brain barely looks up from its e-mail. It sneers: *Is anything ever really free?*

13 Ways to Know You Need Help

1. Your dog nags you. Whines urgently in her throat. *Come to bed, come to bed.*
2. You find yourself saying, aloud, "In a minute, just a minute." You keep tapping keys on your computer, your face washed in blue light.
3. One minute turns into ten turns into an hour and another. You're searching for something but you don't know what. So many voices out there, demanding your attention, so many things that can be done. The lure of websites that promise, just one more, this next page will solve everything, but you don't even remember what you traveled here to solve.

---

3. Nothing important ever happens in the last five minutes.

4. A Cornell Box resurrects what would have been lost: a key to a forgotten lock, a button, a coin, a shell, a seed pod—all these objects that litter a drawer, jumbled, dirty, but put together through intuition and a longing for harmony become something else: a story that layers time, everything existing all at once, all of it contained. I'm tempted now to jump on the Internet and find some interesting factoid about Cornell to insert right here in the essay, something that will relate so coyly and perfectly to the idea of arrangement, but I just, thirty seconds ago, turned off the wireless in order to concentrate.

4. By the time you do wrench yourself away, you feel wounded and confused, as if your brain has literally been torn, shreds of it sticking to the screen.

5. You feel confused by the state of your house. Somehow, in the hours you spent online, the pile of dishes in the sink has grown, the trash has overflowed, clothes have strewn themselves on the bedroom floor. How did this happen?

6. You find yourself in front of the refrigerator, holding open the door, with no earthly idea why you're there. You go to wash the dishes, but find yourself eating a bowl of cereal instead. And now you're sitting in front of the television, watching a rerun of *The New Girl*.

7. You want to be a New Girl.

8. When you finally make it to bed, your dog looks up at you, her face a familiar mix of adoration and accusation. It's a face that says, *Oh, you again, how kind of you to join us*. A face that says grumpily, *Where have you been?*

9. Admit nothing. Just shove her over to her side of the bed. You've done this every night for years, but every night she acts as though it's an affront. She sighs. She's very disappointed in you. You know things are bad when you've disappointed your dog.

10. Promise you'll do better from now on. You'll practice good "sleep hygiene" (as your doctor puts it); you'll brush your teeth, drink a cup of herbal tea, turn off all screens hours before bedtime. You'll do your yoga breathing. You'll stretch a little, put on lavender-scented moisturizer, think only good thoughts. You'll keep a tidy little dream journal by your bed, pen at the ready.

11. Instead, you fall into a fitful sleep, exhausted, as though you've been in a fight.

12. Your sleeping mind skims the surface, like a search engine, lighting here and there, dwelling in the places that get the most hits. You can't settle. You wake too early, more tired than before.

13. You look over at your dog, who sleeps with her eyes open. She sees you but doesn't see you. Her legs twitch. She chases something in her dreams.

Alone, Not Alone

I'm single, and I live alone.[5] Because I live alone, when I come home the dishes that were in the sink that morning have settled there and grown crusty, the floor is still unvacuumed, and no one has cooked dinner. I look accusingly at the dog and the cat, both of whom have done nothing all day. They look back, all innocence: *What?*

"You couldn't lift a finger?" I ask. "You couldn't do a dish?"

Of course, all this muttering, like the insane old lady I'm becoming, substitutes for real human interaction. And it means I go onto my e-mail, Facebook, and other message boards to simulate this interaction all day and long into the evening.

When you live alone, you have no other eyes (at least human eyes) to reflect back to you a picture of yourself, and that's why you start looking elsewhere: to Facebook and e-mail and blog stats, just to feel as though you're being seen *somewhere*, somehow, but it's a funny way of doing it: so disembodied, when it's the body that craves attention. We find our homes filled with voices and conversations that evaporate when we look up. Or are those nebulous relationships just as solid now as embodied ones?

You swim each evening in this disincarnate world, occasionally coming up for air to notice the dirty dishes in the sink and the cat who needs to be fed, and the dog who is sighing into her paws. You could get up and make a phone call to your mother or a friend, to hear a real voice, but no, you sink back down into the tepid waters of the Internet, let yourself float there a while, your eyes flitting from one thing to the next, craving a mild commotion to greet you at the door.

---

5. NPR tells me that I'm part of the fastest growing demographic there is (it's good to feel a part of something). I listen to NPR in the morning, afternoon, and evening. There's always some voice in my ear. I half listen while doing something else. I know half-truths about a lot of things in this world. But I can never remember what I hear. I start too many conversations with phrases like: "I heard this story on NPR, I can't remember exactly what they were talking about, but it was, you know, about that *thing* . . ."

Blog

So you start a blog. A blog about the conundrum of living online and in the real world at once. A blog about being a writer, a homeowner, a teacher, a yoga student. You say your blog will be a letter to the world, becoming like a latter-day Emily Dickinson: "Here is my letter to the world that never wrote to me."

But you are not Emily Dickinson. Sure, you can pull off the recluse act for a little while, but what you really want is the world to talk back to you. And talk and talk and talk.

You post something on your blog. You're a little too proud of this little post. You've found clever pictures and you've written the post in short little digestible chunks. You have a beginning, middle, and end, but it's not too long. You've read all about how people read online. You know they will skim. You have to put things in **bold.** You have lots of   space. You underline and you cross out.

And then you wait. You post and refresh the page. You tell everyone on Facebook: *hey, read my blog post!* You tweet it. You check for comments. You walk away for five minutes, then hurry back and check again. You look to see if anyone liked it, gave it a thumbs up.

You try to do other work, but all your work takes place on the same screen where your blog lurks. It's impossible to get away from it. It's become your pesky toddler, demanding attention. Or maybe *you're* the toddler, saying, *Look at me, Look at me!* You try to swim inward but keep gasping toward the surface, looking for someone to save you.

Marrow

I want to write something that wonders.[6]

But I can't because all my screens are open at once. I'm all fact and surface. My eyeballs swivel in their sockets, try to look inward instead. A laser gaze, down into the esophagus, between the ribs. Beyond the bones to the marrow.

---

6. The space for wonder has shut down, with our hardly being aware of it; as soon as someone says "I wonder . . ." the smart phones get whipped out. The space between knowing and not-knowing has shrunk to the size of hair. Where are the gaps? The long stroll toward an unexpected truth?

Marrow: sweet, salty, dense. You have to suck it out or dig in with a small spoon. It takes some patience. It won't yield easily. You have to spend some time: focus, scrape, close your eyes to taste.

Marrow lives in the furrows, in the deepest part of you. It regenerates. You never see it until a bone breaks. But we live our lives carefully, tiptoeing along the surface, keeping what we can keep intact.

Writing Then, Writing Now

Writing used to be private. Writing used to close the door, say *Excuse me*, wouldn't wash its hair for days on end. Writing put on no lipstick. Writing avoided eye contact, gazed at its toes, mumbled one-word answers when asked.

Now Writing has become gregarious. Writing wants an audience. Writing wants to practice in front of the mirror.

Writing used to moon about, hugging a pillow. Writing used to lip-synch to Simon and Garfunkel: *I will lay me dooooowwwwnnnn . . .*

Now Writing does karaoke. It gets up on the bar to dance.

Writing used to wait. Writing used to be patient. Writing had to go to the library, open the wooden drawers of the card catalog. Writing walked its fingers along the yellowed edges. The library, quiet. The library like the inside of a body, where something gestates.

Now Writing asks questions in a loud voice. Writing snaps its fingers in the library. Writing strides into the library and demands answers. The library hums. There is nothing like silence in the library. There is no body, no gestation, only spontaneous births.

Truce

I've been on many, many writing retreats since that first long retreat at Hedgebrook, but the nature of retreats for me has changed gradually over the years. They've grown shorter, for one thing (thank god), and I often now go on writing retreat with a friend, at a place called The Whiteley Center on San Juan Island, where we fall into an easy routine, supporting one another in our work. I'm finding that I no longer need to see writing as a purely solitary act; in fact, I can get too mired in myself.

And now it's rare to find a writing retreat where Wi-Fi is not on tap.

I resisted this for a long time, stubbornly trying to maintain inner quiet, but I always succumb. I think this sense of being constantly connected has changed what I write—I don't really know if I could write an essay like "Basha Leah" again—but new forms emerge when I do a dance with technology rather than try to wrestle it to the ground.

For instance, the last time I retreated to Whiteley, I stayed for a mere five days.

And in that time, I ended up writing an essay called "36 Holes," and I wrote it almost entirely while glued to the Internet. I was watching a live video feed of the rescue of the Chilean miners who had been trapped underground for months. I watched, I cried, I wrote, I watched some more. I couldn't tear myself away from the Internet, so I allowed the Internet to tear into me.

I thought about holes. Holes that yield treasure and those that do not. These holes accumulated as I watched the earth burp forth the missing. I kept writing them down. I rearranged them. I created a box to contain them.

And something new was forged in those five days: a peace treaty, perhaps, an inching toward a truce between outward and inward connection.

Troubled Water

I'm in my bedroom listening to Simon and Garfunkel sing "Bridge Over Troubled Water." Years from this moment I won't actually be sure that it's Paul Simon or Art Garfunkel,[7] it may have been Bread, or Carole King, or any of those bands from the early 70s[8] who sang of longing and friendship

---

7. I always empathized with Art the most: he was the geeky, quiet guy, providing backup. He looked to Paul to take the lead. But I knew, within him, there yearned his moment in the spotlight. If I allowed myself on the Internet right now, I would insert some relevant fact about the first solo album Garfunkel released—I would find its name and somehow connect that name with the project I'm undertaking now; I would try to download tracks; I would follow a trail that would probably lead to a dead end, but there might be a line or two I could glean. But I've turned off the Internet. I'm here with just my geeky self, remembering an even geekier girl hugging a pillow and wailing, *I will lay me dooooowwwwnnnn* . . .

8. Oh, how I long to look up the 70s! What marvelous details I'd encounter: the hair, the cars, the television shows! It's all waiting for me there: a treasure trove, a Free Box. I want to rummage. I feel it itching there in my fingertips.

and pain with such earnestness. But that doesn't matter, because for now I'm listening with my eyes closed, my hand in a fist over my heart, and I'm exquisitely alone.

The chenille bedspread is a prickly massage on the backs of my thighs. The air has settled into the stagnant pause that occurs after my mother has vacuumed, the whole house smelling of dust unsettled and Pledge. Now my mother might be sitting at the kitchen table with the newspaper, or outside watering the lemon trees.

Like a bridge over troubled water . . . Somehow, though I'm just ten years old[9] I know about troubled waters, but I don't know how one becomes a bridge across them, or to woo a Paul Simon to sing me over to the other side. I suspect there are troubled waters elsewhere in the house, turbulent rapids, though the roar is distant and muted.

When you're weary, feeling small . . . Weariness should be a grown-up feeling, I know this even then, yet here weariness lives, sighing through my bones.

I want my mother, and I don't want my mother. There it is. Caught between the desire to be alone and the desire to be connected. A gap I'll inhabit the rest of my life.[10]

The smell of Pledge. The dust, a taste in my mouth. My mother obliterating all traces of dirt, scrubbing the sink clean. I hear her now, the faint sound of water running into a pot, the refrigerator door opening and closing with its soft whoosh. I can taste stuffed cabbage, the tang of sauerkraut.

Years from this moment I'll want my mother. I'll be vacuuming my own house or swiping down the dusty coffee table with Pledge, or making tomato sauce—and there she'll be, a mother at the bedroom door, listening to the faint melody of "Bridge Over Troubled Water." I'll look up from what I'm doing and say to the dog, "I've got to call my mother," and just then the phone will ring and I'll pick it up, and she'll say, "Hello, it's your mother."

---

9. Am I ten? If I had the Internet on, I would look up the release date of "Bridge Over Troubled Water." But I have to rely on my shoddy memory instead. Perhaps I'll look it up later, if I remember. But these days, if I don't do something at the *exact* moment I think it, it never gets done. The memory cells are diuretic. They flush out input almost immediately.

10. And into that gap rides the Internet, with its promise to be the bridge: Alone → not alone. Isolated → connected. In two places at once.

I want to be a bridge over troubled water, but this bridge is built plank by plank, a suspension bridge that hangs improbably midair. It looks like it could never hold the weight of a single person traversing side to side, not to mention two or three or hundreds of people chattering in your ear.

It's the kind of bridge that would vanish in an instant.[11] Like the movies I watch, where the heroine makes it, but the bridge disappears before the villains can traverse. She now finds herself alone on the other side.

I'm on your siiiiiide . . . And I've somehow decided—in that room, the record spinning in its wobbly way on the pink record player—that I must shoulder everything alone, even in the midst of family. Even while my mother makes dinner and waits for me to open the door.

Free Box

I sometimes think about writing this way: as though I'm still standing on a porch decades ago, the heavy lid in my hands, rummaging and rummaging, until some unexpected thing winks at me, tells me to pick it up, examine it for what story it can tell. Or not a story, but merely what role it might play in calming down the connective tissue in my brain. Focus it. Making everything a little more clear.

During those Orr Hot Springs years, I wrote in a notebook until a Brother word processor arrived via UPS: a clunky white machine that allowed you to type and see four lines at a time on a tiny, dim screen before those lines transferred to the page. It seemed like a miracle, but at the same time a little odd: processing words the way we processed basil in the Cuisinart for pesto. It was slow writing, like slow food: not meant to be gobbled quickly.

On the porch at Orr Hot Springs, there wasn't much to distract you but your own mind. Sure, you had your to-do lists, but that list included taking a long soak in the morning, followed by a sauna and a swim. You ate breakfast while reading a book, because we didn't get a daily paper. We listened to a staticky radio station that broadcast from the Bay Area. We talked and talked and stopped talking. We chopped wood. We cleaned bathrooms. We drank tea

---

11. As a kid, we walked on such a bridge somewhere, and my brother, as kids do, swayed it from side to side. I laughed in my terror, trying not to gaze at the turbulent waters below. My mother held my shoulder in a death grip.

made with weeds. We turned compost over with pitchforks, the smell ripe and promising.

So you had a lot of brain space to fill with your own musings. A brain full of ideas both big and small and everything in between. And that Free Box kept standing—solid, immovable—ready to offer what you needed. I go there now, pick up the heavy lid, smell the damp wood, the musty interior. *To you the earth yields her fruit*, Kahlil whispers to me from his perch on the Internet, *and you shall not want if you but know how to fill your hands.*

DINTY W. MOORE

RIVERING

Rivers have been used as a metaphor for storytelling perhaps as long as stories have existed. Rivers start small, flowing forward toward an end that can't be seen before arriving, and rivers insist on finding their own way to that unseen end, carving through whatever soft sand, hard clay, or rigid shale is found lining the banks.

I teach nonfiction writing at Ohio University, the first public institution of higher learning west of the Ohio River, in what was once called the Northwest Territory. The university dominates the city of Athens, along a bend in the Hocking River.

Narrative flows. Narrative meanders. Narrative changes speed. Narrative thickens in spots and grows thinner in others, deepens here and turns shallower there. Narrative takes whatever it finds and carries it downstream.

> I've known rivers: I've known rivers ancient as the world and older than the flow of human blood in human veins. My soul has grown deep like the rivers.
> —Langston Hughes

For twenty years I've taught storytelling—creative nonfiction writing—to college undergraduates. My students understand terms like character, setting, plot, and dialogue from the first day, but all of us in the room struggle when it comes to what "meaning" means in a work of literature, or, as they like to call it, identifying the "theme" of a piece.

What does a story *mean?* How does it mean? Where does the meaning come from? Who put it there? How do we know if we've got it right?

Some students approach a work of literature as if it were a dictionary entry or a puzzle. Once you figure out what it means, you can close the book.

"Theme" is even worse, from my perspective. It suggests a moral lesson, inserted by the author, usually a dead white author, something about man, or nature, or religion, or perhaps an immense symbolic creature of the sea.

The Hocking River was once called the Big Hock-hocking River, or the Hocking Hocking River, or the Hakhakkien River. A few folks in town still call it the Hockhocking, the name most common in the nineteenth century and the one I prefer.

Try it, out loud. *Hockhocking.* It catches in the back of your throat, like the echo in a cave.

The name goes back to a Native American word, meaning shaped like a gourd.

The river looped, and cut back on itself.

The river told a story.

A few years back I devised my own metaphor to replace "meaning," my own way of trying to guide young writers to acknowledge the intuitive vapor of emotion, metaphor, image, and idea that makes a piece of creative nonfiction—an essay, a memoir—more than just a collection of scenes or observations, something greater than the sum of its many parts. How does a piece of writing open up into something wide and powerful, or reflect a truth that is "older than the flow of human blood in human veins"?

The term I chose was Invisible Magnetic River.

Every good story, to my mind, has one.

The Hocking River used to flood into the city of Athens on a fairly regular basis. In 1907, the flooding was especially bad, sweeping away twenty homes, scores of cattle, and killing seven people. Less damaging floods came along year to year, until 1968, when the river reached another record crest, so severe that it destroyed not just homes but a number of buildings on the Ohio University campus.

Students, it was reported, could dive out of their dormitory windows into the water. And they did.

Invisible. Magnetic. River.

Why that first word?

Because thesis sentences are dull, flat, and awkward.

Because once you say a thing out loud it will often become less potent.

Because a truth you discover for yourself will always be more powerful than a truth someone else tries to impose upon you.

Because in an essay, or story, or poem, the truth is sometimes not in the words, but between them, in the permeable tissue that runs from moment to moment.

Because sometimes, more often than you think, even the author isn't fully aware of the meaning.

> Eventually, all things merge into one, and a river runs through it. The river . . . runs over rocks from the basement of time. On some of the rocks are timeless raindrops. Under the rocks are the words.
>
> —Norman Maclean

Magnetic.

Because everything—words, images, scenes, snippets of dialogue—everything on the page—should be drawn toward the river. Pulled down, gently.

Not snapped into place. Not forced into a straight line, but urged, encouraged to lean in toward the river's flow.

Because if the moment on the page does not lean in toward the river, it does not belong in that essay.

Because if there is no magnetic pull, no current, then all you have is words.

> Every really good story, no matter how short or how long, carries something of its justification for being and all its attendant parts in every single line. It is a unified created work of word art and that is why it is so difficult to do.
>
> —Richard Bausch

In 1969, the Army Corps of Engineers began rerouting the Hocking River, with funding from Ohio University, so that the campus could expand without running an annual risk of high water and flooded buildings. So that students would no longer dive out dormitory windows.

A new river channel, with three times the carrying capacity of the old one, was etched on the edges of the town, changing the very geography of Athens, keeping the river well-contained.

For now, the river only flows where the engineers have said that it can.

> The river itself portrays humanity precisely, with its tortuous windings, its accumulation of driftwood, its unsuspected depths, and its crystalline shallows. . . . Barriers may be built across its path, but they bring only power, as the conquering of an obstacle is always sure to do.
>
> —Myrtle Reed

Say it: Hockhocking.

The engineers managed a rather graceful curve in the new riverbed, but it doesn't feel natural. It can't be mistaken for the unpredictable, sometimes elegant, sometimes abrupt, always idiosyncratic way that a river actually cuts through a landscape. It feels too much like what it is: man-made.

We do, of course, have a firm hand in shaping the stories we tell. Our initial ideas, false starts, and occasional moments of clarity become the underground springs that feed the stream, form the river. We are the ones filling the channel with water, after all, one bucket, one keystroke at a time.

But just as nature builds a better river, the invisible magnetic flow that gathers beneath our words and sentences, once this flow gains tangible momentum, will tell a better story, find a deeper truth. The emotional, or intellectual, current, if we are attentive, will begin to suggest words, and those words will conspire to finish our sentences for us. Those finished sentences will ultimately tell us what we're thinking, or what we've learned.

The struggle for the writer is to follow the river, not force it. The struggle is to trust the invisible current to carve through whatever soft sand, hard clay, or difficult truth is encountered; to carry us all, writer and readers, downstream, to that unseen end.

BOB SHACOCHIS

HOW TO WIND THE CLOCK OF YOUR DAYS: NOTES ON THE NATURE AND FUNCTION OF TIME IN THE NEW MILLENNIUM

1. Get a dog. Kids will work for awhile, especially when they're babies, going off like alarms right on schedule, but as they grow up they become unreliable, begin to oversleep and apparently lose their ability to tell time or even pretend to harness a healthy respect for time's verities. Don't get a cat. Cats only acknowledge one setting on the clock—the food setting—but otherwise don't give a shit about time. What happens if the dog runs away, or worse, dies (like in Milan Kundera's *The Unbearable Lightness of Being*)? Then time stops, and when time stops, you're either on psychotropic drugs, you're dead yourself, or you're very very sad. But nothing on earth braids together the two fundamental strains of time in your personal universe with such tidy eager harmony as a dog.

2. A problem with Kundera's novel—it made me cry, as I recalled the deaths of my own beautiful clock-winding dogs over the years. This is not relevant because good books and arty things are not supposed to make a sophisticated, overeducated audience cry. This is relevant because it's common knowledge, or so I have reason to believe, that broken hearts cannot tell time. Broken hearts are blind and senseless to time, skewered on a cruel white hot spike of stopped time, writhing, oblivious to the count of the days, because what's the point of counting when one never leads to two and two never flips ahead to three but is just one, one, one.

3. I'm thinking right now that one one one might very well be classified as a third state of time, but essentially there are just two types that we all roll with—Big Huge Time and Itsy-Bitsy Time.

    If you prefer fancier more dignified names, try Macro-Time and Micro-Time, which are the terms I use in the classroom to try to explain this stuff. Or try some more comfortable nomenclature, Cosmic Time and Real Time, although Real Time, at least as we encounter it on the page, is an illusion, and Cosmic Time is not. No matter the nomenclature, both kinds of time, strangely enough, have a paradoxical quality in which they can masquerade as the other—Big Huge Time can pass by you at the speed of light, and a moment in Itsy-Bitsy Time can occasionally stretch into a blissful or bloody eternity.

    Orgasms and car wrecks seem to share this capacity.

4. Perhaps like most of you or some of you or none of you, my schooling in these two types of time began before I was a writer; specifically, when I left the country in 1973 at age twenty-one and ended up in the Caribbean, living and working with a spearfisherman by the name of Raimundo Lung. Years later, when I wrote about Mundo as a character in my short stories, I couldn't bring myself to give him a made-up name, because in life, Mundo was already larger-than-life. He was a genuine clairvoyant—not something that I easily acknowledged or readily accepted as a white kid from the suburbs. But Mundo was in the habit of falling asleep and dreaming and when he woke up he would share his dreams with the people around him and the dreams would be prophetic, be about the future, and whenever he told me one of his dreams the dream invariably came true. After I went away from the island where I lived with Mundo, I didn't see him again for twenty years, and when I finally saw him his son smiled knowingly and said he and his father knew I was coming back soon because Mundo had dreamed my reappearance two nights earlier.

    When was the last time you dreamed of me? I asked Mundo. I never dreamed of you in my life, he said, until two nights ago. Don't think Mundo's prescience doesn't bewilder me. It does. But it doesn't make me a cynic. Hollywood (and Toni Morrison) likes to tease us with magical negroes, but I never saw Mundo as a magician or a sorcerer. He just lived more intimately with nature than anyone I've ever known. Living that close to nature apparently has its benefits.

Perhaps your wiring connects with a different set of sensors.

5. My life in the Caribbean as a young man was constantly pushing this information at me: that time has not one shape but two, and its cosmic shape is amorphous, porous, filled with wormholes, popping up here and there and everywhere, everything happening all at once, past, present and future. You might recall that Einstein, in his doodling days, had a similar vision of time, which came attached with a thousand blackboards' worth of chalky equations. It is the habitat of memory and hope, and the kingdom of dreams. Time's other shape, chronology, is a donkey, a beast of burden, plodding forward at the steadiest rate, one foot in front of the other, minute after minute, day after day. The writer can choose to be Mundo or choose to be the donkey but if the writer chooses to be both, which is actually a normal state of affairs, the writer better be a master of the craft of artful, coherent, graceful transition between Big Huge Time and Itsy-Bitsy Time or the writer will fail.

6. There are also two fundamental types or states of existence—flesh (or matter) and words (or ideas/emotions). We are told that in the beginning was the word, ideas outside of time, and then, somehow, the word was made flesh, and flesh, as you know, is a hapless prisoner of time. So, the question arises: Is time structure, or just a relentless stringing together—*structure* being an entity implicit with meaning, *stringing together* being an activity implicit with coincidence, meaningful or not?

Is it possible to relate this basic dynamic of our life in the cosmos to a publishing problem? Yes. More about that in a minute.

7. During the very first information revolution, when prehistory became history around 3400 BC in ancient Sumeria and Egypt, the first attempts to make language visible—to make language written—had little to do with time except in its most static form,

recording the death of a king or the birth of a child or the date of a battle. Mostly, writing was accounting, a function of commerce and the marketplace. Twenty units of wine, thirty goats, sixteen slaves bought or sold in my master's house. (By the way, we count as the Babylonians did, using sixty fingers—seconds and minutes.) "Writing as a carrier of narrative"—meaning writing as a vehicle for containing the orderly passage of time—"did not evolve for another 700 years in the Sumerian epic tale of Gilgamesh" and the ancient flood. (And also by the way, time-wise, the Koran gets this story of the deluge right and the Bible doesn't. As a matter of fact, whoever was keeping time in the Old Testament must have been drunk.) But starting with Gilgamesh, to tell stories, human beings had to invent a different, more plastic way of thinking about time. In short, they had to formally, consciously, manipulate time, which primarily meant shrink it, without screwing up its credibility, its verisimilitude. Time, for the first time, became a deliberate artifice. And without that evolution, literature would not be literature but some exhausting and unrealistic attempt at documentary. What I mean to say is, once the limitations of Real Time were set aside, Cosmic Time was invited in as a partner in the storytelling. [Facts courtesy of *New York Times*, October 20, 2010, "Hunting for the Dawn of Writing," by Geraldine Fabrikant.]

8. Gabriel García Márquez: "Life is not what one lived, but what one remembers and how one remembers it in order to recount it." Translation: Life, reflected, is not found in Real Time, but in Cosmic Time.

9. In the early 90s, I spent about eighteen months on and off in the field in Haiti, chronicling the invasion of the island by the US military. When I turned in my manuscript to my editors at Viking— there were a bunch of them—their response was that this was not the book they had been counting on me to write. We were expecting a policy book, they told me, and were very disappointed. I had delivered to them a literary narrative. I had given them flesh (in time), when what they wanted was ideas, unanchored from time, except in the way time can be used as a marker, referring to other

markers, but not integral to a cause-and-effect pattern of meaning the way time functions in a story. Within a very short time of its publication, Viking knocked the book out of print, and I decided to write (withdraw into) a novel for the next ten years, where I imagined I could have my way with Big Huge Time and Itsy-Bitsy Time, utilizing them—exploiting them—as I fancied, without being kicked in the seat of my pants by editors.

10. How Not to Sell a Memoir. Four years ago, or maybe five, the wonderful writer Debra Monroe finished a memoir, *On the Outskirts of Normal*, about being a single white woman in southwest Texas who adopts an infant black female. Debra's my friend, she sent me the manuscript, I knew she had gotten rid of her ineffectual agent, and I suggested she send the manuscript to a well-known New York agent who represents Michael Cunningham and Scott Turow and Julia Glass and so on and so forth. The agent loved the manuscript but said no one at the NYC publishing houses would ever publish it because it had a nonlinear timeline and publishers believe that no matter how well a memoir is written, a nonlinear timeline means no sale. Debra, rather than jamming the narrative into a straight chronology, had let her memory write the book, and as you know, memory works organically in Macro-Time, dipping in and out of Micro-Time like a hummingbird to create scenes, vignettes, anecdotes as needed. She tried and tried to revise the book according to the agent's and the publishers' parameters. Two years later it was qualitatively a better book but the timeline still had bends and twists and loops in it, and it was rejected by the people known as the best editors at the places known as the best houses. I helped her find another agent who was for personal reasons absolutely enthralled by the memoir's subject—there was a genuine connection between the agent's family life and the narrative of Debra's book. But, same story. Timeline is too confusing for a general audience. Read the book though, which was published by SMU Press and praised by critics, and that's the last thing you would feel, that the timeline is difficult to follow. What's the moral of this story? I find it too depressing to even think about.

11. Do you think the way I've structured these remarks is phallocentric? Jab, jab, jab. If I didn't structure these remarks but just let them fly, would you think that was somehow effeminate? Is it possible that I've both structured these remarks and simultaneously let them fly? Is there something about the sun rising in the morning and setting in the evening, day after day, that you find too linear and simplistic and banal? Is there something about remembering the sunset from five years ago as you drink a glass of wine watching tonight's sunset that's too confusing?

12. Charlie Baxter, in his *New York Review of Books* essay on Jonathan Franzen's most recent novel, *Freedom*, asserts that "Franzen is a writer of great patience. This is his glory and his curse."

    A few lines later, Baxter says, "Readers like David Shields whose time sense is more irritably prone to aesthetic boredom have found Franzen's novels to be too slow, too filled with experiences, to reflect contemporary life." Franzen has a voluptuous sense of time that reminds Baxter of nineteenth-century English and Russian novelists. Franzen himself in the novel seems to speak directly to critics like Shields. Here's the excerpt:

    > It's the same problem everywhere. It's like the internet, or cable TV—there's never any center, there's no communal agreement, there's just a trillion little bits of distracting noise. We can never sit down and have any kind of sustained conversation, it's all just cheap trash and shitty development. All the real things, the authentic things, the honest things are dying off.

13. "Our perception that we have 'no time' is one of the distinctive marks of modern Western culture."   —Margaret Visser

14. Maybe time is one of those real, authentic, honest things that are dying off. The smartest insight I heard anybody say at the turn of this current decade came out of the mouth of Leon Wieseltier, the literary editor of *The New Republic*, in a commentary published in the *New York Times* that attempted to come to terms with the first, lost decade of the twenty-first century: "Attention deficit disorder

is no longer a disorder in America. It is a norm. Attention is now the disorder."

15. Tom Friedman, in a column of his own a few months later, colored in the pathology: "We've become absorbed by short and short-er-term thinking—from Wall Street quarterly thinking to politi-cian-24-hour-cable-news-cycle thinking. We're all day traders now. We have day-thinking politicians trying to regulate day-trading bankers, all covered by people tweeting on Twitter." The paradox is, of course, that the faster we stuff our heads with information, the less we care about that information, and the quicker we devour it, forget it, and move on, which would be perfectly fine if we were a plague of locusts and information was an endless crop of corn. Eat, eat, eat, die.

16. Sam Anderson, the *New York Times*, 12/31/2010: "It would be hard to dispute that over the last 5 or 10 years, the culture's relation-ship to time has changed pretty drastically. The shift is so obvious that it's boring, by now, even to name the culprits: Google, blogs, texting, tweets, iPhones, Facebook—a little army of tools that have given rise to (and grown out of) radically new habits of attention. Many of us are now addicted, on the dopamine-receptor level, to a moment-by-moment experience of life that's defined by a behavior sometimes referred to as 'time-slicing': jumping every few seconds between devices or windows or tabs, constantly swiveling the peri-scope of our attention around and around the horizon to see where the latest relevant data-burst might come from." Translation: We all now reside in the Land of Crazyfuck.

17. When time gets out of control, stories fracture into incoherence, and a culture starts to disassemble from the center. I don't really care if accelerated time, spinning and flailing time, time smashed into a million bright splinters, is an accurate reflection of contem-porary life. I'd prefer to play the fool, whether in *King Lear* or on *Comedy Central*, the agent whose role it is to hit the pause button, and trick the players into reflection. Sanity and meaning cling to time, Big Huge and Itsy-Bitsy, both of which have a natural rhythm

that provides a basic component for our humanity. When a writer nurtures this sensibility, when she reaches out and gathers up and weaves together the fullness of time, something marvelous happens as Cosmic Time and Real Time seem to meld into a single unit—I'm thinking here of Jennifer Egan's *A Visit from the Goon Squad*.

18. I recently lectured at the Bennington Writing Seminars, on the occasion of my sixtieth birthday, about the making of an American writer—specifically, me. The math I conjured for my audience was simple, and its simplicity breathtaking: four times sixty equals two hundred and forty. Let me explain the profound significance of these numbers.

Imagine this. The topography of northern Virginia, where I grew up, rises westward from where the Potomac River slides past Washington DC toward a ridge about twenty-five miles out of town and if you stand on that ridge on a clear day you can look northeast down Route 50 and Dolly Madison Boulevard all the way to the rooflines of the capital and turn and look west to the nearby skyline of the Blue Ridge Mountains. On July 21 of '61, the ridge was lined with cannon of the Army of Northeastern Virginia, aimed at nearby meadows and farmland surrounding a place called Manassas Junction, cut through by a small river named Bull Run. Perhaps one hundred yards from the long row of cannon stands a Confederate drummer boy, dressed in butternut trousers and gray blouse and forage hat squashed on his head. He is ten years old, terribly excited, and when the artillery batteries fire the opening salvo of the first major battle of the war the drummer boy is permanently awestruck by the shattering thunder of the rounds and the howls of armies hurtling themselves toward one another. He has never witnessed anything more spectacular or thrillingly grand in all his life, and believes he never will again. But the year is not 1861, it's 1961, and the drummer boy is me, costumed out for the centennial reenactment of the First Battle of Bull Run. What I remember most from that day, besides the sinister magnificence of the cannonade, was (is) my father leading me into a circle of rebel soldiers to meet at its center three old-timers who looked like grizzled Santa

Clauses. A century before, their own fathers had fought in this very war, the War Between the States, and my father nudged me forward to shake their hands. It's a tableau I feel a great reverence for—a child of Camelot, raised inside the Beltway, shaking hands with the children of our nation's greatest tragedy. Add two more generations to the equation—one a child and one a very old man—and you've time-traveled right this instant through flesh back to an America that had yet to produce its Revolution. Two hundred and forty divided by four equals me. The duration of my own life has thrust this revelation upon me—I have finally understood the youth of our country, our country's youthfulness. And have finally understood that in many ways I have lived in lockstep with that youth, and that it's over.

19. We're not indulging in magical thinking here. A writer named Robert Krulwich cataloged this taffy-pull phenomenon of personal/ historical time, Big Huge Time and Itsy-Bitsy, recalling in his NPR blog how in 1973, in a Brooklyn deli, he struck up a conversation with an old man who had grown up in St. Petersburg, Russia, during czarist times, and the old man's neighbor had been the mad monk, Rasputin, who was assassinated in 1916. There are people who live long enough, Krulich wrote, "to create a link—a one-generation link—to figures from what feels like a distant past, and their presence among us shrinks history." The blogger Jason Kottke likes to collect examples of what he calls "human wormholes"—people who help us leap across space and time.

   • Samuel Seymour, when he was five years old, witnessed the assassination of Abraham Lincoln, and in 1956, Seymour was interviewed on television about his memory of the event.

   • Supreme Court justice Oliver Wendell Holmes lived long enough to shake hands with both Presidents John Quincy Adams and John F. Kennedy.

   • President John Tyler, born in 1790, has two grandsons who are still alive today in 2012.

- Three Civil War widows lived into the twenty-first century, even collecting the pensions of their husbands, veterans of the Confederate Army.

The elasticity of time, so available, so intimately accessible, seems to me to contain some elemental code that might help us understand what it means to be an American, yet I find it odd that many—most?—contemporary American writers seem to shy away from it, or at least isolate it into well-wrapped packages. Historical novels. Futuristic novels. Novels of the moment, for the moment, by the moment. Nothing wrong with that, but where's the sweep, the stretch, the intermingling?

20. Stephen Burn, the *New York Times*, 12/31/2010—"Seated on the cusp of the network revolution, the critic Sven Birkerts catalogued the losses that a reader in the electronic millennium would suffer: divorce from historical consciousness, a fragmented sense of time, a loss of deep concentration. From the other side of the divide, the ability to locate a cluster of like-minded people must seem a real gain to the reader who finds isolation uncomfortable rather than one of reading's fertile preconditions. Yet however the economy of costs and benefits is calculated, the change in technology that organizes the audience changes the rest of the writing world. Some writers may try to seal themselves off from the crackling energy of the Web, but the contemporary novel's form is always a model of the way our minds work, and it registers the deep changes in the ways we process data. A contemporary novel offers an opportunity to measure fiction's mutating forms—to note, perhaps, the dominance of time as a thematic obsession in the works of the last 20 years, or the emergence of the family epic."

21. I guess it's about time I talked about *The Woman Who Lost Her Soul*, the novel I began in 2002 and finished in December of 2011. As I've said elsewhere (note: I'm a hearty practitioner of the faux crime of self-plagiarism), the book is a monster—almost 900 pages, set on three different continents, with four separate but interlock-

ing chronologies, each backdropped by a different war, with I'm sure more than ten but I think less than fifty characters (it's not that I've forgotten the number—I've never actually counted them).

When I finished the book, the manuscript spent the next six months in the hands of two very excellent editors, one a professional paid by my publishers, the other a friend and former student of mine who asked to read my final draft and just went ahead and edited the damn thing in a most brilliant fashion. Both editors had their own ideas about how to trim some of the tonnage off the beast, yet they both surprised me by agreeing on one issue that I didn't see coming—they wanted to delete any sentence that violated standard operating procedure for chronology. For instance, a sentence like this:

"That New Year's Eve was the last time he ever danced with his mother, who, two years later, would succumb to pancreatic cancer."

Or this: "The next time Dottie Chambers saw Tom Harrington, in another time and place, he would understand that what had happened between them in Haiti had been no accident."

Both sentences, as you can see, invite the future into the present and past, and thus allow themselves, and the consciousness of the voice, a more expansive sense of time. For me it's mostly a voice question—I like what happens to the sound of a sentence when the breeze of the future ruffles the language. Neither editor, however, had much tolerance for the technique. Wow, I told them, it's a good thing you guys didn't edit *A Visit from the Goon Squad*, a novel in which individual scenes have their dramatic payoff, but the power of the aggregation of the scenes depends entirely upon the author's sensibility about time, Big Huge and Itsy-Bitsy.

22. EDITOR: I'm reading *A Visit from the Goon Squad* and stand by my assertion that I don't have a knee-jerk reaction to flash-forwards, just a certain kind of flash-forward.

ME: Ah, well, if she does the flashing better than me, that cuts me, hard.

EDITOR: She does a different thing entirely. I think what I was cutting from your book was those teaser flashes. All that stuff about what would eventually go down "up north" in the plotting. And I just said cut it back, not cut it altogether. That kind of stuff you have to have an exceedingly light touch with or it feels like you're dragging the reader along by his nose. And, more to the point, your narrative already had mucho momentum without the flash-forwards. Her flashes aren't teasers, aren't related to suspense or momentum. They're . . . I don't know. Building a sense of tragedy or pathos or something?

ME: Her flashes are—I'm going to coin a word here—chrono-thematic. Her structural sensibilities mirror mine—the eternal present, which contains both the past and the future. Although it's true, and you're right, that many of my flash-forwards were teasers, and I'm sure some of them were just thrown in to remind me where the fuck I was headed.

23. Here's what I mean about the consciousness (and sound) of a voice being chrono-thematic. This is an excerpt from an essay about swimming by Sven Birkerts:

> Maybe this is why I've never really written about "swimming" before: I find just too many layers bound up with too many different things. It goes so far back. Long before there were pools and meets, there were the years at Walnut Lake, starting with the earliest times of growing up and then, later, the period when my father thought he would train me and turn me into a competitor. All these phases are still somehow with me every time I take that first time-obliterating plunge. To fix on this timelessness feeling is paradoxical, I realize, given how much of my swimming was for years about the opposite, about clock-time: getting through whatever distance as quickly as possible. But this is not the swimming that matters anymore, though the memories of that still haunt with every stroke. What matters is the other, the lake and pond swimming, when I can feel my whole existence peeling

away from me—I felt it again just this morning: I set my glasses aside, waded a few feet into the shallows, and then dove. All time, no time, everything just silvery bright bubbles and light and skin sensation, and every stroke I took after I reached the surface again was just a coda for that.

24. In Greek mythology, Kronos was the god of time, and I see him reincarnated here in Birkerts's essay, a young swimmer leaving the shore, his strokes like clockwork, the rhythm a type of mantra, *We're starting, we're starting,* and that same swimmer now an old man, returning to shore, the rhythm the same but the mantra different, *We're finishing, we're finishing.*

    Or I imagine Kronos morphed into a version of himself more recognizable by David Shields—a shaven-headed and tatted-up god, fond of crystal meth, surfing the channels at a rate measured in nanoseconds. Or Jennifer Egan's Kronos, commanding a goon squad of course, dressed in black ninja pajamas, kicking down your door at midnight.

    My Kronos is a holy trinity of dogs—Petey, Emma, and Sissie, each born knowing how to wind the clock of my days. They keep time perfectly, Big Huge Time and Itsy-Bitsy Time, and, as a favor of love, they keep me from getting lost in time. They really do.

    Who wants to get up right now and go for a walk?

REFRESH

I watched *Vertigo* in college, because I was in college and it was the sort of film you were supposed to watch. I liked it well enough and promptly forgot all about it. But for whatever reason, the film has recently resurfaced from the morass in my brain where old movies go to die, and so one night I biked down to retrieve a copy from the nearest locally owned video store (that is, I streamed it on Netflix). As you may know, it's a very weird movie. At its heart is Jimmy Stewart's obsession with Kim Novak, which isn't much of a mystery if you've ever seen Kim Novak. But I found myself marveling at the cinematic crispness of Stewart's obsession. Here he is trailing her to an old Spanish mission, and an art museum, and San Francisco Bay. Eventually the two of them fling body against body against the moody wet backdrop of a redwood forest. Oh, sweet release.

But it was the quieter moments that drew me in: Stewart tailing her in his car, or awkwardly interrogating the owner of an apartment house. The potential dangers behind every door, the frantic dread of losing Novak in traffic or the cold indifferent waters of the Bay. And studying Stewart's face—pallid and sweaty, creased with hope and anticipation and fear—I realized that I'd had those same feelings not so long ago, but my obsession didn't look anything like his. It didn't look like much of anything.

I envy *his* obsession, the narrative satisfaction of it. But it's 2012. It's hard to get there from here.

So this is a story about a girl, and of course any time a guy says that it's a dead giveaway that it's really about him. Okay, it's about me. You know my name, and I'm not going to tell you hers. But I've come to detest bland pseudonyms. If you've got a story about a girl named Lara and change her name to Anne, what's the point? You may as well go all out. This is my story about Ms. Clarissa Applesauce.

Some background: In the fall of 2008, I moved from Denver to eastern Kentucky to take a job teaching English at a small university that will go unnamed. Due to the particulars of regional heritage (whatever that means), Nom de Guerre, KY, was in no sense a College Town. It was, rather, a typically sad rural town that happened to have a university within its city limits. I took a small studio apartment just off of Main Street—a block of mostly empty stores kept that way by the two families who had owned it for decades and were determined to keep the twenty-first century (and much of the twentieth century) from intruding upon the bucolic calm of their Appalachian paradise. I lived across the lot from Main Street's most lucrative business: a drive-thru liquor store that opened at 7:00 AM and did a brisk business with the early risers.

Thus did I find myself marooned in a foreign land far from home, and it seemed the perfect time to embrace my inner ascetic, that contemplative monk I'd always sensed dwelling deep in my chest who would only come into his own if forcibly divorced from the din of constant and easily accessible stimuli. I would live, if not like Thoreau, at least like my literary heroes from the twenties: Hemingway, Fitzgerald, Nate West, John Fante—whatever their faults, none of them had to endure the ignominy of finding themselves clicking mindlessly on a link entitled "Keira Knightley Goes Shopping."

So I declared my life television and Internet free. I had my music, my books. In this grand fantasy, I saw myself hunched over in my walk-in closet of an apartment reading Proust and Tolstoy, maybe even *Finnegans Wake*. Why not? We all know one hour of unperturbed silence has as many minutes as three or four hours of random Internet puttering or stupefied television viewing. Come eastern Kentucky or high water, I too would live deliberately.

In retrospect, I view this experiment as a scientific one: can a man survive for an entire year feeding on nothing but delusion?

Because, of course, once stimuli were gone, I missed them terribly. Whatever the ultimate benefits might be of plodding through *Remembrance of Things Past,* they in no way could compete with the free and depressive clarity of clicking from website to website, seeking something, anything, to temporarily distract my brain. My daily routine went like this: teach in classroom, hang out in office with the magical "Internet" that existed there, come home to throw oneself down on bed or floor. Either nap or stare at ceiling. Eat. Return to office till midnight, drown self in Internet. Reflect on life. Contemplate buying volleyball to talk to. Without a scintilla of evidence to the contrary, pretend tomorrow will be different.

Tomorrow: repeat today.

I lived like this for nine months. But then (cue upbeat hopeful emo song), I met a girl—the aforementioned Ms. Applesauce. I struck up a conversation in Nom de Guerre's only coffee shop, which was actually a small alcove off the town's only bookstore. She was reading *Slaughterhouse-Five*. In what can only be described as my smoothest pickup line ever, I asked her if she liked it. She referred to it as a great "cuddle-buddy." I still have no idea what this means. But conversation ensued and numbers were exchanged and we planned to meet for a drink a few days later.

I was a new man, and spent those intervening days in a whirligig of euphoria. I walked up and down the bombed-out streets of Nom de Guerre dreaming of all the adventures that awaited us—road trips to Nashville and Asheville, star-spangled nights camping out in the Smoky Mountains or romping through the cheap tourist paradise that is Gatlinburg, TN.

These flights of fancy were ridiculous, but they sure beat lying on the floor counting the speckles in the ceiling.

I suppose I could draw out our first (and, spoiler alert, *only*) date, paint a colorful scene and detail the social anxieties and social cues and social et ceteras. But let's not. The bare bones go like this:

1. She brought three friends. They talked in a closed-circuit about people I'd never met and events I hadn't attended.

2. Besides her friends, she knew about 78 percent of the other patrons. (If you were born in eastern Kentucky, it's apparently impossible not to know at least two-thirds of the people in any given room.) They swallowed her up.

3. She got really drunk. I got regular drunk.

4. I sat alone at the bar—oh, glorious cliché—for god knows how long and eventually watched her staggering out of the bar with her friends.

5. I walked home.

Cue sad, hopeless emo song.
End of story.

Except it wasn't.

That night was only a prelude to the real story, which began the next day when she sent what I'll refer to as E-mail #1. She apologized profusely, told me she was fresh from an abusive relationship. The abuser had been her fiancé. They'd set a date and everything.

I wrote back something heartfelt and dripping with empathy. I'm pretty sure I included that James Wright poem about wishing words were grass. Thus began our electronic correspondence. She told me she was no good at this; she was shy and nervous. She needed to go slow.

Sure, I said.

I returned to Colorado for the summer. We "talked" via e-mail and text message. I wore out the buttons on my phone crafting exquisitely edited texts. I drafted e-mails, printed them out, and sat outside on my brother's porch late into the night revising until they were just right. I gently pushed for a phone call, but she had a thing about talking on the phone. It was too . . . immediate. Too close. Uncontrolled.

Sure, I said.

And of course it was weird, and unorthodox. But those adjectives are right up my alley. Who wants a nonweird orthodox girlfriend?

She convinced me to join Facebook, which up till then I'd successfully avoided on the basis of some vague, hard-to-explain principle. Sort of like the Indians who feared cameras could flash away their souls. But I was in the long grass now, and I guiltily clicked on her photos and Older Posts. My mother had taught me from a very young age not to be the kind of person who rifles through people's drawers when they're not home. But this was a new kind of house—windows wide open, not a locked door in sight. Or like a diary left open on the coffee table, adorned with a Post-it note that screamed READ ME!

So I did.

I pondered every male face for hints—which one of these yokels was her erstwhile fiancé? Which were potential suitors? I took mental notes of her likes and dislikes, which didn't disappoint. She liked *The Godfather* and David Bowie in *Labyrinth*. She loved Bob Dylan and obscure underground bands I'd never heard of. If my friends had invented a girl to torment me, they couldn't have done much better.

And still came the e-mails and text messages—every day, every other day. She'd text me when she was tromping through the mud on her parents' stamp of eastern Kentucky soil; she'd text me when she had a nightmare. She sent YouTube links to songs, snippets of philosophy. I studied her e-mails and texts as though I could uncover hidden nuance and meaning—the lonely kabbalist at work. They couldn't just be words. Too much was riding on this. "Too much," naturally, being the omnipresent fear of another year of wretched Appalachian solitude.

We made plans to meet again when I returned to Kentucky in August.

August came. E-mail #58 (all numbers are approximate) contained plans to meet for a hike. Two days later, Text #2,144 introduced a reason to delay. I would hear nothing for a week, then be greeted one fine morn by an e-mail explaining that some minor catastrophe—ex-boyfriend drama, sick grandfathers, the weather—was to blame. And we'd start over.

I grew impatient and ever more confused with her excuses, which were legion and rarely creative. My only excuse, presumably, was desperation. To be fair, I was desperate. But also intrigued. She *was* smart, and interesting, and damaged in some irresistible Sylvia Plath (or, if you will, Fiona Apple) way that fed my admittedly naive Savior fantasies. This was 2009, remember—a time of hope. I was the change she'd been waiting for.

Each new message was the proverbial shot of adrenaline straight into my atrophied heart. When two or three days passed without hearing from her, I grew restless and sunk. I'd send a text, and wait. Then a follow-up text. And wait. I'd send an e-mail, and wait. And wait.

She seemed to have an otherworldly ability to gauge my level of frustration. As soon as I was ready to completely and irrevocably be rid of her there would come the familiar Pavlovian vibrating beep of a new text message to just barely renew my battered hopes.

Parry, thrust.

Step forward, step back. Make plans and break them.

This went on for over a year.

Let's not draw this sad story out any longer. But rest assured that I didn't quit Facebook the first time I tried. And I couldn't quit her. I knew it wasn't healthy, but more than that, it felt like I was being jerked to and fro by a girl and a relationship that didn't even exist. An unhealthy relationship I could handle, because at least it would pass the time. But this was metaphysical humiliation. If a normal face-to-face relationship is a simple (or even not so simple) math equation, then this was some abstruse mathematical proof full of symbols you've never seen before. Or else pure gibberish.

I'd erase her e-mails and texts, and resolutely tell myself not to contact her or respond when she, with the painful regularity of an iTunes service agreement, butted her electronic head back into my life. My resolve would crumble as soon as my phone started to buzz or I'd see her name pop up in the e-mail tag.

I don't know what else to call it, if not an obsession. I don't think Jimmy Stewart had anything on me. But I couldn't explain it to my friends, or hardly to myself. The fact that it was playing out on a virtual stage was beyond humiliating. There was no "there" here. I rebuked myself for feelings that weren't "real"—how could they be? Real things happened in the real world, a place of trees and tables and sidewalks and sticky barroom floors. This was happening exactly nowhere.

Eventually she just stopped. Eventually I moved on. But what this odd not-love affair from an odd time in my life spurred me into thinking is this: so much of life today—its victories, defeats, confusions—now comes to us in ways that seem tremendously uninteresting. Even if I filled the long spaces between texts and e-mails with local color (and eastern Kentucky has plenty of that), it wouldn't change the fundamental fact that this massive and consuming event in my life was taking place on a stage bereft of what we would traditionally consider tension and drama. I was sitting in my office checking my e-mail, or sleepwalking through my days until my phone buzzed with an incoming text. Pathetic might be a word I'd use, but dramatic it was not. Nor was it evocative, or resonant, or any of the other chipper workshop words we use to describe effective prose.

The great premise and promise of creative nonfiction is that—regardless of a few minor costume changes—these things are True. They happened to us, and they matter. But they also have to be interesting. What happens when our reality becomes not just somewhat, but remarkably nondramatic? What happens when the conduits through which our emotions flow seem frivolous and somehow beneath mention among civilized people?

Beneath us they may be, but they're still here. And they won't be going away anytime soon.

In the first act of *Vertigo*, Jimmy Stewart trails Kim Novak to the art gallery in the Palace of the Legion of Honor in San Francisco. We get the establishing shot: Ionic and Corinthian columns and a Roman arch. Very classical, very classy. Inside, Stewart squints at Novak, who sits prim and stiff on a bench and gazes up at a painting. A bouquet of pink flowers lies beside her. She wears a cold gray dress-suit. Stewart strolls behind her in his gangly way, in his ill-fitting brown suit, with his furtive glances. He holds his brown fedora loosely with both hands. Novak's hair is pulled back in a coiled French twist. The background music works to heighten the sense of thick museum silence.

No words are spoken. No words need to be spoken. And though *Vertigo* is, obviously, a work of visual fiction, that scene plays out in countless iterations countless times a day, in public spaces all over the world. A man looking at a woman. Deep feeling—lust, heartache, trepidation, hesitation, irritation—conveyed through fleeting glimpses and body language. No direct dialogue is necessary.

Clarissa Applesauce and I had words; it was all we had. Words sent to one another through the ether, through broadband and Wi-Fi. Words that presented themselves out of a void. Words without accompaniment, without context or environment to inform or enrich them. Words, words, words. The transcripts would total hundreds of pages, but they wouldn't add up to anything approaching a compelling or enticing narrative.

Give me a rider on horseback passing love letters from one end of town to the other. Certainly I'll paint you the local color: trees in full bloom or autumn rags, the wind through the rider's hair or rain slanting violently down. The breathless gallop of the horse. But I'll also give you the clanging of the bell announcing his arrival, the sky behind him as he stands framed in the doorway, his outfit, awkward greetings and pleasantries, the passing of the letter, the tactile feel of unfolding the envelope, a sense of the handwriting.

We're worlds away from that, of course. But even a phone call has its awkward pauses, stumbles, tonal shifts, accusations, affirmations, endearments, silences, frantic pleas, or the jerky breathlessness of pacing around a room. I can do that. And I can do the meeting of eyes across a crowded party, all gestures and posturing; or a walk through the park; or even the quick freighted brush of knee against knee beneath the table in a pizza parlor or coffee shop.

But in the end, I haven't the slightest idea how to write in full dramatic flourish of the highs and lows of my virtual Appalachian romance. And though I've since engaged in more traditional, "normal" (not to mention healthy) relationships, even these couldn't be honestly rendered without the ways in which emotion in this second decade of the new millennium is bound up irrevocably with communication systems that didn't exist a generation ago. A fun first date is validated with a text good-night, or a friendly e-mail the next day. Burgeoning relationships are punctuated with flirty and affectionate electronic missives, many of them containing grammar mistakes, truncated words, fatuous emoticons. Fights play out through the same satellites and wires. Who wants to read about that? And who wants to write about it?

As far as I can tell, the answer is no one. The answer for most writers is to hit the IGNORE key. Which may be a feasible option, I suppose, for writers of fiction. Just pretend it doesn't exist in our lives. Create a 2012 fantasyland where the characters act like it's still 1992. Pretend, as they do on television, that drivers and passersby and coffee shop patrons aren't all acting as though they have advanced OCD, or like addicts who can't go five full minutes without chasing the virtual dragon. This is the new normal. This is how we live.

Of course, not every event in our lives needs documenting. I've never felt cheated when a memoir doesn't take bathroom breaks. But this omission feels different. We are engaged in a deliberate bout of wishful thinking, an almost childish game of "Let's pretend." Most people I know under forty (and that's most people I know) dive into the Internet first thing in the morning. Even my friends who pride themselves on their hyperactive lifestyles—bouldering, skiing, rafting dangerous rapids—will plug back in as soon as they've finished their playdate with nature, and still spend significant hours of their days in front of a laptop or hunched over the computer that lives in their phone.

Significant is the operative word. Shouldn't these modes of communication be recognized for the multifarious and important functions they serve in our lives? Can they be, in any way, interesting? And if our creative nonfiction can't find a way to integrate this great and/or sad truth about how we spend our days, what does that say about our craft? Maybe we're just fiction writers in disguise, sweeping under the rug what we find distasteful or shallow or boring about modern life in order to tell those truths that we find more elevated, more heightened, less embarrassing. Just reach for the preordained grace notes. Follow the old script. Aim for the same rote moment of clarity or flash of insight. One more tired epiphany on top of a mountain.

And to be honest, if I encountered a character in an essay or memoir who spent a significant portion of his days checking e-mail and reading texts—who acted as many of us act—I would almost certainly laugh. How preposterous he seems, grasping after his silly gadgets. A caricature, really. A flat one-note joke.

I don't have a solution to this problem.

I read somewhere that one of many reasons *The Simpsons* is considered such a landmark achievement is because it was the first show to portray a family doing what families had been doing for decades: lounging around and watching TV. But that's satire. It's comedy. And while I might be able to successfully render my "unreal" relationship with Clarissa as pure farce, it wouldn't be True. Maybe it was a farce of sorts, this connection built on clipped text messages and sitting alone in rooms at my computer waiting, waiting—god, the waiting!—for the next thrust of virtual contact, but there was also passion and anxiety and hope and desperation and secret sharing between two damaged souls.

And none of it was funny.

As a postscript, I should probably mention that I received an e-mail from Clarissa about a year ago. She was attending vet school on an island in the West Indies. She just wanted me to know, she wrote. She described how it felt to drift off to sleep at night listening to the ocean, to wake up listening to the ocean, to walk barefoot on the white sands near the ocean. All that crap.

I composed my response as concisely as possible: *Glad to hear it. Be well.* But I couldn't bring myself to stop there. What was the point? I asked her. Was there a point? Did any of it mean *anything?*

It wasn't a rhetorical question. I really needed to know.

She got back to me in less than an hour. *I wrote all about it in my diary,* she said. *I don't want to rewrite it all. Send me your address and I'll send the pages.*

I doubt I can successfully convey just how gratifying was the promise of a tangible letter. I might never see her again, but answers were coming. The pages, either heavily bonded and fancy or thin and cheap, would be torn, neatly or in haste, from a diary bought at some high-end craft store or maybe Walmart. The pages would be covered in tidy printed script or cramped cursive, written with ink from a pen she had received as a gift or maybe cribbed from a motel. A pen she had actually held in her small and almost chubby hands, which I remember being oddly and cutely out of proportion to her thin frame. The pages would come in an envelope she'd sealed with her own spit, the lipped fold of the envelope pressed shut with the tip of her finger. The letter would travel physically from an island halfway across the world. It would pass through the hands of uncaring strangers. One day, jetlagged and road-weary, this letter would arrive in my curbside mailbox. I would separate it out from bills and coupons. I would hold it in my hands.

Anyway. I'm still waiting.

ROBIN HEMLEY

LINES THAT CREATE MOTION

About two years ago, I spent three weeks at an artists' colony in Virginia, and one Sunday morning, several of the other writers and artists in residence decided to go for a drive. In one small town, we saw a sign for an estate sale. I love such sales, even though there's a voyeuristic, even slightly ghoulish element to the venture, but then writers and artists tend to be a curious lot. We decided to stop and take a look around. I didn't plan to buy anything, but you know how these things go. Within half an hour, I was loaded down with various items I hadn't realized I needed, among them a silver mechanical claw for extracting olives from a bowl and a scrapbook compiled by a stranger, presumably the one whose estate was being sold, dating from the 1940s. A scrapbook, as its name implies, is a compendium of scraps from a life, usually the ephemera commemorating various milestones in the life of the person who owns the scrapbook: wedding announcements, birth announcements, theater programs from memorable evenings out on the town, that sort of thing. But in this case, the scrapbook was much more than some newspaper clippings and such pasted onto construction paper. This scrapbook had belonged to a woman named Mary Hilliard Wilson, who was born in Easton, Pennsylvania, in 1919, three years younger than my mother, and whose scrapbook covered the years 1940–1947. Apparently, another such scrapbook existed or exists, but it was purchased before I arrived at the sale. I wish I had arrived in time to buy that one as well. This scrapbook contains not only the usual ephemera of the milestones of Mary Hilliard's life, but is more like a time capsule, containing among its other treasures, an x-ray of one of her teeth, her birth certificate (we share the same birthday, May 28), the nylon stockings she wore throughout the War, a newspaper announcing the Allied invasion of Normandy, the button from a uniform of the bomber pilot she dated, her American Red Cross pin, her employee evaluation from her stint as a volunteer taking care of shell-shocked servicemen at Walter Reed Hospital in Washington, DC, even some handicrafts made by her patients at the hospital. In short, there were just enough of the artifacts of a life lived during a particular historical epoch to intrigue, but not enough to illuminate. I knew when she was born, where she'd gone to school, her employers, the holidays she'd taken in Mexico and in the Caribbean, the memorial window for her parents that she'd sponsored at her local church.

Of course, I was not her intended audience. She had compiled this text for herself or for her future children or grandchildren, of which I believe she had none. How had her romance with Robert, the bomber pilot, ended? She'd pasted among other memorabilia a telegram from him saying he was visiting Washington and wanted to see her, and then nothing, no more mention of him, but instead, thirty-four pages of the scrapbook devoted to her trip to Mexico with two of her girlfriends. Had Robert broken her heart? Was the trip to Mexico her consolation prize to forget him, to put him in the past? And what about that page of the scrapbook in which a wedge had been deliberately cut out? What had occupied that space?

Before I try to answer that question, let me take you to a scene from my own life.

I'm twenty-one years old and sitting in a café called the Runcible Spoon in Bloomington, Indiana. I'm seated near the front door—it's the type of place in which patrons share tables, but I'm seated alone, near a potted plant, facing the espresso machine and the front counter. I'm writing in my journal, trying to figure out how to look like a writer rather than trying to write. A group of four or five gathers by the front door, peering outside, one of them my waitress. "What's going on?" I ask.

"It's Borges, of course," she says, as though Jorge Luis Borges always comes into the Runcible Spoon. In fact, it IS Borges. My professor, Willis Barnstone, one of Borges's translators, has brought Borges for a monthlong visit to campus to deliver a series of lectures. Until this moment, I had forgotten the exact dates of his visit and now he's here. As Borges makes his way up the path, guided by a graduate student, the people gathered by the door disperse, resume their studied nonchalant poses at their tables. Someone lowers the music a bit. Act natural, the patrons of the café seem to be thinking in unison because everyone looks so unnatural, including me, as the front bell tinkles and Borges makes his way inside holding onto the arm of the student who glances around and sits him down in the closest seat to the door, which is directly across from me. The waitress appears immediately at the table and Borges and his companion both order espressos in my memory. Of course, Borges is blind and at best I probably appear to him as indistinguishable from the potted plant beside me, and I am just as responsive as the plant. Borges is my literary hero. I am a comparative literature major and all my favorites are works I read in translation: Kafka, Isaac Babel, Mikhail Bulgakov, but none of the authors have ever sat down across from me at a table. What can I say to him, my literary idol?

Again, please pardon me while I leave, for a while, my twenty-one-year-old self trying to figure out what he could possibly say to Borges that might sound halfway intelligent. I'm not sure why I want to say anything to Borges except that in the presence of greatness, I'd like to say something, to fix myself in his mind for even an instant, to hitch a ride in his consciousness for a moment.

My parents were both translators of the work of Nobel laureate Isaac Bashevis Singer. In fact, though both were prominent writers variously of poetry, short stories, and novels in their day, they're most well known for their translations of Singer. But my parents didn't really translate in the literal sense. Neither knew much Yiddish, and certainly not enough to translate. Singer or his nephew would make a rough translation of the work, and then my father would sit down with Singer and Singer would tell him what he was attempting to convey. My father, as a poet and novelist, would then recraft the sentences, spending as much time in this re-creation as on his own work, if not more. You might say that he was a trans-editor rather than the translator because he never knew the original, but in a sense he had unprecedented access to the original in that he often had the author sitting right in front of him, and he could chat with him in the way that we would all wish to chat with our favorite authors when we really love a book, as though he or she were seated right across from us in a café.

As readers and as writers, we're always engaged in some form of translation or another. Most of us do not, indeed, have the writer of the original sitting across from us, as my father did with Singer, as I did with Borges. In my father's case, he was able to ask Singer intelligent questions. But what did I do with Borges sitting right in front of me? I couldn't think of a thing to say, not a thing. Of course what I wanted to say was, "I love your writing," but what is the translation of that? I think "I love your writing" could be translated simply as "Notice me," or "Bestow some of your grace, your genius upon me," or perhaps something equally trite. It doesn't matter. The idea is easily translatable, the idea of being without language, of being inarticulate in the face of wanting simply to engage.

For quite a while after this nonencounter, I felt that I had missed a great opportunity, but then I started to view the experience a bit more philosophically, perhaps a little in the manner of Borges himself. After all, this is the essential problem of being human, that we are each stuck inextricably in our own consciousness, and try as we might to understand one another, we most often fail miserably, except when the artist successfully translates what is going on in her consciousness into the mind of the reader. And then perhaps we feel somewhat as I felt sitting across a table in a crowded café from Borges. I perceived Borges or some representation of him, and he, being blind, could not perceive me. Isn't this the experience of reader and writer, the writer vaguely aware of the shapes out there of his audience, but unable to see them clearly, while the reader feels as if he could reach out and touch the author, if only. If only.

Because of my family connection with Singer, I could, if I wanted, speak with him directly, but such encounters are inevitably disappointing. In 1981, when I was a student at the Iowa Writers' Workshop, I gave him a call at the behest of the director of the Workshop to see if Singer might come to Iowa City for a reading.

"Hello," he said.

"Mr. Singer. This is Robin Hemley."

"Robin Hemley. What happened to you?"

"Nothing. I'm at the Iowa Writers' Workshop."

"Are you married?"

"No, that's my brother, Jonathan."

"Which one are you?"

"Robin."

"So how is your writing?"

"Great. I'm having a wonderful time here."

"And what is your brother doing?"

"He's in L.A. He's an electrical engineer."

"Is his wife there? Is she a nice girl?"

"She's there, and yes, she's very nice. I just called to say hello and ask if you might give a reading here."

"This year, I'm very busy, but I would like to in the spring."

"That would be wonderful, Mr. Singer."

"Call my secretary, Deborah. She's a nice girl."

"Great."

"And Robin, how old are you?"

"Twenty-two."

"Twenty-two. My Gott. How time goes quickly by. You know this thing your brother did, becoming an engineer, is very good. Publishing is bad these days. If you want, you should become an engineer like your brother."

So, you see, sitting across the table from our favorite writers, as it were, can be a disappointment. It's much better to engage them with the barrier or the safeguard of translation between us. Yes, the safeguard of translation. Why is it that writers who write in other languages besides English inevitably interest me more than writers in my own language? Is it simply exoticism that draws me to Sebold, Borges, Kundera, Babel, Chekhov, Bulgakov, Cortázar, Márquez, Fuentes, Kōbō Abe, Tanizaki, Proust, and yes, Singer, instead of, say, Philip Roth and Saul Bellow? No, I love many American writers, English, Australian, and Canadian writers, too. But I relish the inherent ambiguity embodied in the translation. When I'm rereading Proust, as I'm doing now, which translation do I opt for? The Moncrieff or the more recent translation by Lydia Davis? Is the most recent necessarily the best? The most accurate? And what do we mean by "accurate?" I'm fascinated by the way a translation has the ability to constantly renew a text. The poems of nineteenth-century poet Henry Wadsworth Longfellow, once a staple of American literature, sound rather tedious and unintentionally comical in English at this point, especially this terribly dated offering of stereotypical Native American.

> By the shores of Gitche Gumee,
> By the shining Big-Sea-Water,
> Stood the wigwam of Nokomis,
> Daughter of the Moon, Nokomis.
> Dark behind it rose the forest,

> Rose the black and gloomy pine-trees,
> Rose the firs with cones upon them;
> Bright before it beat the water,
> Beat the clear and sunny water,
> Beat the shining Big-Sea-Water.

But perhaps this is gorgeous in Polish? Or Yiddish?

Even this, I think might be renewed by a good enough translator.

In Borges's classic story "The Aleph," two literary rivals hold the pettiest of literary feuds despite the fact that in the basement of the house that belongs to one of them, rests the most remarkable object in the universe, a window that allows the viewer in the right position to view every space and object in the world at once. These petty rivals might be all-viewing but they're not all-knowing. The rival of the fictionalized Borges, Carlos Daneri, is the most mediocre of poets who squanders his gift of the aleph by writing a poem that is a kind of lyric cartography of the world, a poem deadly dull if minutely accurate. In a sense, all writers have this aleph in front of them, and some do no better than Daneri. It's not a matter of what one sees, but how one sees it, and who is doing the seeing. A Russian translator told me that the reason so many works of English and American writers are admired so much in Russia is due to the fact that some of Russia's greatest authors have historically had a hand in translating these works. Pasternak translated Shakespeare. Dostoyevsky's first book was a translation. Brodsky translated John Donne. And Alexander Sumarokov has a warped translation of Hamlet, "wonderfully intrusive" in the words of another friend of mine who is also a Russian translator, in which most of the characters do not die. I have not read this translation of Hamlet, but I'm glad it exists. Its existence doesn't negate the original, but adds to it.

"You should read this in the original," people sometimes say about works that I will never be able to read in the original, and there are times when I feel wistful that I cannot read Proust in French or Bulgakov in Russian, but even if I could read the original and you could as well, would my experience and yours be the same? The original exists beyond the words on the paper or screen. They exist in the mind of a long-dead author, and what we get are many translations. When I read James Joyce's famous story "The Dead" when I was nineteen, I was reading a different story from the one I read when I was thirty. The first time I encountered the story, it had no impact on me. The second time, I found it beautiful and devastating. You might say that it wasn't the story that changed, but that I changed, and of course that's so, the receiving end of any work of literature, the reader, is in a constant state of flux, and so what she apprehends on one day will not necessarily be what she understands on another.

When I look at translation in this way, I see that there are at least four types of translation that interest me: from language to language, from lived experience or the writer's mind to the written form, from one discipline, say, photography, to another, and from author to reader. It seems to me that as writers, no matter what we're engaged in, we're engaged in a form of translation.

In the early 1960s, the American short story writer Flannery O'Connor, on a visit to the University of Chicago, prefaced her reading of her story "A Good Man is Hard to Find" by discussing charges against her own fiction that she wrote in a grotesque manner that purposefully distorted observable reality. "I don't believe that any serious writer approaches a subject or a scene with the intention of creating a grotesque effect," she stated. "I believe that the writer who is any good at all intends what he writes to be neither naturalistic nor grotesque but literal. A good story is literal in the same sense that a child's drawing is literal. When a child draws, he doesn't aim to make anything appear distorted but to set down exactly what he sees, and as his gaze is direct, he sees the lines that create motion. The lines of motion that interest the serious writer are lines of spiritual motion as they can be perceived on the surface of life and followed deeper in to some point where revelation takes place."

Words such as spiritual and revelation make some of us put up our guard, myself included, and while I don't share O'Connor's Catholic faith, I am rather obsessed with these lines of motion, of arresting them for a moment, and trying to perceive more than the blur of life. This is part of why Mary Hilliard's scrapbook intrigues me.

Still, there is always the risk that what we create will in fact be perceived as grotesque, especially if we have no idea of the lines that create motion in the original. Take, for example, the lion that King Frederick of Sweden purchased in 1731. When the lion died, its bones and pelt were sent to a taxidermist who had never before seen a lion. The result was both hideous and hilarious, a cartoon of a lion that delights and repels me in equal measure. While the Lion at Gripsholm Castle is a travesty of a lion, it is still a fascinating travesty, and I for one, am perversely pleased that it exists. Its existence in no way negates the existence of real lions.

As for the truly literal-minded, the people who think there is an original to which they must stick, though the original is often troubled and in contention, I admit I sometimes feel a bit disdainful. A quote often misattributed to the Texas governor Ma Ferguson has her declaring, "If English was good enough for Jesus Christ then it should be good enough for the children of Texas." It's a delicious quote, even if apocryphal. Likewise, I feel impatient when writers and readers are literal-minded in their expectations of form and genre. When Moses descended from Mt. Sinai, he wasn't carrying the genres in his hands, but some people act as though he did. If language and interpretation are fluid, then certainly so is form. The hybrid is almost always more inherently intriguing and exciting than the form of expression that stays within proscribed boundaries. And so, I'm attracted to forms of literary expression that borrow from one another freely: the essayistic piece of fiction, the poetic, the prose poem.

Several years ago, I wrote an article for *New York Magazine* and for the first time in my life, a professional photographer was assigned to follow my every step through the day. Jeff Mermelstein is widely considered one of the finest candid street photographers in the world. Jeff only uses film—no digital photography for him, and even had an assistant alongside him whose sole job was to load his cameras and rewind and label film. I hit it off with Jeff and a couple of years later we were chatting on the phone about a forthcoming book of his, titled *Twirl/Run*. The book comprised two photographic subjects, men and women running in urban landscapes (many seemed to be late, hurrying somewhere important) and women twirling their hair. The two subjects seemed to have nothing to do with each other, but he felt the photos belonged together and he was looking for an essayist who could create an essay that would in a sense translate the photos. I asked him if I could give it a shot. I love such challenges—it's the challenge of the poet who marries two disparate images or ideas and creates metaphor. Of course, Jeff's photos accompany the text. It was my intention for the photos and text to speak to one another, but not serve merely as simple illustrations. But does this make such an exercise fiction instead of nonfiction? I don't think so. A large portion of our lives is spent daydreaming, thinking about future scenarios, about possibilities. If we refuse to allow speculation into the essay then we're closing a door on an important aspect of our lives, the philosophical realm.

Roland Barthes in his classic study of photography, *Camera Lucia*, uses two terms, *punctum* and *studium*, to describe our reactions to photographs. The *studium* can be translated as what the photo represents in aesthetic and intellectual terms, wholly disconnected from our emotional response. The *punctum* can be translated as the *wound* of the photograph. It's both emotional and individual. The *punctum* for you might be different from my sense of the punctum in a photograph. It's a small detail that wounds us, a boy's crooked teeth in a photograph of a group of smiling boys, a man shading his eyes from the sun in another.

Camera Lucida was his last book, written not long after his mother died. The book is an elegy for his mother camouflaged as a book on theory. He describes searching for a photo of his mother shortly after she died, one that would capture her essence. For the most part, the search was fruitless until he came upon a photo of her and her brother as young children standing on a bridge in a glass conservatory. He calls it the Winter Garden photo. When the photo was taken, both his mother and his uncle's parents were going through a divorce. He describes the photo but refuses to reproduce it in his book. He writes: "I cannot reproduce the Winter Garden Photograph. It exists only for me. For you, it would be nothing but an indifferent picture, one of the thousand manifestations of the 'ordinary'; it cannot in any way constitute the visible object of a science; it cannot establish an objectivity, in the positive sense of the term; at most in would interest your *studium*: period, clothes, photogeny; but in it, for you, no wound." He couldn't be more wrong. In fact, his description is so poignant that of all the photos in *Camera Lucida*, it's the one I best remember. What he has created is the *punctum* through words. For me, the *punctum* is the awkward way in which he describes the way his mother clasps one finger of her younger brother's hand, in the way that children sometimes do.

I knew nothing about Mary Hilliard when I purchased the sliver of her life represented by the scrapbook. I view her life as the original and her scrapbook as a self-translation, though I do not have the advantage that my father had with Singer of being able to ask the author questions for clarification. Mary gives up very little. I know the jobs she had, the dances for soldiers she attended, the weddings she attended (none of them her own), the bomber pilot named Robert whom she seemed to have dated briefly, her stint as a Red Cross volunteer at Walter Reed Hospital in Washington, DC, her compassion for the shell-shocked boys she looked after in Ward 24. But the scrapbook ends abruptly, unlike her life, which lasted another sixty some years beyond the war.

Why have I become obsessed with her? Well, isn't this the question at the bottom of much of creation? I suppose it has something to do with the fact that she and my mother were contemporaries. Perhaps Mary is a stand-in for my mother, who has been dead since 2004. The longest section of the scrapbook illustrated her postwar vacation to Mexico with some of her girlfriends. My mother visited Mexico at the same time as Mary—this was the logical place for Americans who weren't wealthy but had some means to visit after wartime travel restrictions were lifted. My mother went there to finish her novel, but she also fell in love with her own flying ace, a former RAF pilot in World War I, a Texan named Elliot Chess, sixteen years her senior.

Mary's TRIP TO MEXICO! takes up thirty-four pages, at least a third of the entire scrapbook, and brims with photos, articles, advertisements, schedules, an immunization record showing the entire course of typhoid and tetanus vaccines she took before and after the trip, road photos, her two girlfriends posed beside a couple of strapping Mexican lads, one wearing a conductor's hat, the other a brimmed hat the size of a Panama. And the captions:

> Beautiful Flat roads
>
> Mexicans really do take siestas.
>
> Look carefully and see:
>
> 1. The plaid seat covering of Anne's car
>
> 2. An Indian woman carrying a baby on her back
>
> 3. Indian hut

In Mexico City, Mary's friend Anne takes in a bullfight, but Mary and Fran catch a movie instead. Mary sampled tequila and eavesdropped in the crowd that took in some "Native Mexican" dances, and she kept a pelota program which featured a photo of a handsome pelota star dressed in white and flashing a dazzling smile. Her favorite sport, she declared, and next time she'd learn how to bet.

Was there a next time? I'd like to think so. My grandmother, a music teacher in Brooklyn for many years, saved her money and took Caribbean cruises in retirement, and my mother traveled to San Miguel de Allende when I was a child to get some writing done away from me and my siblings, and to see friends. I'd like to think that Mary, too, returned to Mexico during her lifetime and filled other scrapbooks, or flipped through this one to remind her of her first big trip. But who's to say?

I suppose that I am, because without me, the intermediary, the translator, there's nothing to tell. My knowledge of the original is certainly suspect—for all I know, I might be creating a version of Hamlet in which not only everyone lives, but in which they break out into song, hug one another, and exchange gifts at the end. Only Mary or those who knew her, now a dwindling number certainly, could tell me for certain how much I'm distorting the original. Still, I don't take the task lightly and I feel that the success of my project relies precisely on how directly I can gaze at the lines that created the motion of Mary Hilliard's life. I'm not after biography here, but significance. I want to be literal to the text in the way that Flannery O'Connor spoke of the literal, and not in the way that we often use the term. It's my task to interpret, not to record, which was Mary's task, but not mine. And then after I'm done, it's the reader's task, if she's willing to engage with my interpretation, to reinterpret. A constant synthesizing of new originals for as long as the work seems relevant to the person performing the translation.

JOE WILKINS

NIGHT

What I remember without qualification is the dark.

What I remember is being pulled from the dark of sleep by my grandfather—I can just see the wide, shadowing brim of his gray felt hat—and placed gently in the sheepskin-lined backseat of my grandparents' Oldsmobile. What I remember is my little brother, his small, warm body next to me, and beside him, my straight-backed older sister. Now my sister, who is thirteen and understands what this is all about, buries her face in her hands. What I remember is being pulled from the dark of sleep and into the dark of deep winter midnight in eastern Montana.

What I remember are the Oldsmobile's headlights carving out the dark, hollowing the space before us: two-lane highway, arms of winter cottonwood, quick flash of a sandrock ridge and the Bull Mountains beyond. Does my grandfather tap the brake as we slip around the ess curves above the river? What yellow eyes are those near the culvert? Jackrabbit? Skunk? Maybe coyote? Is my brother crying now? Does my grandfather park beneath a streetlight? Who allows us entry into the dim hospital? I don't know, I don't know—I can see some way into the night, but no farther.

What I remember is a priest in a black smock. Dry-eyed, the priest holds my crying mother. Why is this priest holding my mother? And did we go, then, into another room? Or was my father wheeled in? I don't know, I don't remember, but anyway here he is—my father, still and cool, on a metal table. The priest bends over him, thin lips moving in prayer. Some part of me wants to say the priest dips his two fingers in a squat, wide-mouthed glass bottle and traces a cross of oil on my father's forehead. In the fluorescent hospital lights, some part of me wants to say I can see the oil shine.

What I remember is my mother touching my father, her hands all over his chemical-yellow body: his stick arms and bloated face, his bald head and sunken chest. What I remember is all of us are crying, even my grandfather. What I remember is it is all too much. We leave. Or maybe my father is taken away. Anyway, we are no longer where my father is, or where his body is, and we are collapsed into plastic hospital chairs, and we are still weeping, though more quietly now, our hands useless and strange as wings in this too-bright room.

We are there a few minutes or a few hours. I don't know. But whether he was wheeled away or was always in some other room, whether we wept minutes or hours, everyone gets up to see my father one more time—even my little brother, whose sodding breath sounds like small, sad bells—and I don't get up, I don't rise from my chair to go with them. I don't go to see my father.

Everyone else goes. I don't go.

I am sad and afraid, and I seem to be alone, I see myself alone. Do they really leave me in that anonymous hospital room? Does maybe the priest stay with me? Or one of the thin, busy nurses? I don't remember.

There is so much I do not remember. And part of me wants to say, what of it? What does it mean, anyway, to remember? If a coyote clacks its yellow teeth in the night, if a cross of oil breaks and scatters the light, if I am alone or not alone—what does it matter? The light broke one way or another. That coyote must be dust. My father is in Montana still and is dust. And me? I am no longer that sad, round-headed boy. No longer, if I ever was, scared and alone. Though I did not rise to see my father, I go about my days and tell myself it does not matter.

Or do I, like a boy, pretend?

It goes like this: my wife and I are on our way home from visiting friends in Chicago. My wife is driving. It is evening, our headlights hollowing the dark along this flat, straight, Midwestern freeway, and I am resting in the passenger seat, my forehead on the cool window glass. Just out of Moline, I see beyond the fence line the quick blink and turn of yellow eyes—and like that I am a small boat drifting back a muddy, snowmelt river of miles and years; like that I am a brokenhearted, fatherless boy in the lonely-making distances of the American interior; like that I want more than anything to rise and look again on my father.

We leave and never leave. We grow up and never grow up. We grieve and grieve and grieve. But sometimes, we turn and face that grief; we sit very still with ourselves and, as best we can, remember. For remembering is the opposite of pretending, it is the beginning of telling the truth to yourself about yourself. In a culture dangerously bent toward the consumption of what's next, remembering becomes an act of resistance, of compassion for the self and for the world.

Yet I know, too—why did my grandfather, gentle cowboy that he was, have his hat on inside; why the anointing then, when my father was already hours dead?—memory is never enough. Memory spins and skitters, winks in the dark. Like an oil slick, memory fails and rainbows the light. The boy needs a story. As does the man who was the boy. For it is in the weaving of a story that the boy begins to understand. That the boy becomes a man. It is in the telling of our story that we most fully find ourselves in the world, that we resist all that would have us shrug our shoulders and give in to some mean and particular oblivion.

It is not easy. We must bring to the work of remembering and storying all that we can bear. We must wonder, analyze, visit, listen, research and read, make metaphor—and then, if we're lucky, we might find the first thin threads, we might begin to twine.

Yet we must know as well that story is a power beyond us. It is something elemental, as necessary as air or a warm coat against the winter wind. For as long as there have been human beings, there have been stories. And we, the tellers of true stories, we must pull hard on each thread—to see that it holds, to test that it is true—for the twining is, always, an imaginative exercise, each loop and slow ravel an act of faith as much as fact, a kind of prayer.

We make stories of our days. All of us. In story—in the informed, imaginative leap from memory to broken memory, from long-ago midnight highway to recent noon-blue birth—we learn to live like human beings in the dark houses of our minds. Beyond anything we can do, we are alone in there. And we rightly spite that lonesome darkness. We reach out, then, with what it is we have, fumble for the hand of the other—mother, brother, sister, stranger, lover, son—give to them our heart, our story.

There is one last thing I remember:

My grandfather takes me in his hard arms. He pulls me up and out of my wool blankets and patch quilt. He sets me, gently, on the edge of the old army bunk I share with my brother. He tells me I must get dressed, but I am sleepy and do not want to wake and get dressed. I try to lie down and curl again beneath the covers. My grandfather does not shake or reprimand me. He simply takes me again in his hard arms. *Your father needs you,* he says. *You need to go now to your father.*

And now—in memory, in story—I do.

BALD IN BACK WITH THREE HEADS: WRESTLING WITH TIME IN NARRATIVE NONFICTION

I poked at the Zen garden in the tiny black box on my colleague's window-sill as we traded frustrations about our current writing projects. "Yesterday I told my students to add more context and perspective to their writing," she sighed, dropping a file folder on her desk, "and this morning, my agent informed me that energy lies in immediacy." I nodded, combing the sand with the little rake. Every long-form creative nonfiction writer I know struggles with time in her work. For more months than I care to count, I'd been struggling to find the right structure for a science-history-memoir. Why was time—so palpable in our lives—so difficult to manage on paper?

I knew what time was, of course. I pictured time as a hand slicing through space, clock hands inching across a flat face, a heartbeat punctuating silence. I told my students the next day that Webster defined time as "the measured or measurable period during which an action or process exists or continues," and that, translated into narrative terms, time is "place" (the space where action occurs) "action," and "people" (someone to observe or take the measure of the place and action).

> I was sitting in a taxi, wondering if I had overdressed for the evening, when I looked out the window and saw Mom rooting through a dumpster.

This relatively simple opening sentence in Jeannette Wall's *The Glass Castle* contains all of the elements of time. The place is a taxi; the consciousness is the narrator wondering; the people are the narrator and her mother; and the movement is the narrator's eye and her mother rooting through the dumpster. There is even a temporal reference—"when." It was not hard to find other examples.

> There was once a town in the heart of America where all life seemed to live in harmony with its surroundings.

Rachel Carson's *Silent Spring* opens with the "once" of fairy-tale time. The place (America) and the people (the town) are immediately identified. And the word "seemed" alerts the reader that all is not well; life in this town is either about to change, or has already begun to change in ways that are not yet obvious.

The class seemed buoyed, but I knew it was temporary. I knew I couldn't explain to them how time actually *works* in life, or precisely how to translate that experience to the page, or why time in narrative nonfiction is similar to but also different than the time of drama or fiction.

The Early Days of Time and Plot

Walter Freeman, a professor emeritus of neurobiology at UCLA, believes that the ability to sense time developed as soon as organisms were able to move, when an organism needed to compare its location "before" a movement, and then "after," in order to propel itself toward food or away from danger. With a primitive olfactory bulb the organism could sense whether a scent surged or abated as it changed position even before there were nervous systems or brains. The primitive "sensing" triggered a cascade of neural firings that pushed the body forward (or backward) in response to a perceived change of scent. The hippocampus, the tiny seahorse-shaped structure housed deep in our brains, sometimes called the "seat of memory," is thought to have evolved from the primitive neural apparatus that held and compared scents.

As animals evolved, so did our talents for tracking, retaining, and retrieving experience. One cannot wait until a tiger pounces to run away. Anticipatory premovement neural firings developed into impulses for fight or flight, pleasure and approach—physical responses embodied in the limbic system that give rise to fear, dread, anticipation, anxiety, excitement, suspense, urgency—and all the other feelings and impulses that prod us into acting. The comparing of sensory data before and after movement blossomed into our notions of "cause and effect."

According to neuroscientist Antonio D'Amasio, our current ability to re-member and predict involves not only the hippocampus, but also areas of the brain that generate visual imagery, enable self-processing, monitor subjective time, assist in narrative structuring, and evoke feelings of familiarity. Our knack for remembering and predicting as we process ongoing information gives us our sense of self-in-the-world. Add language and the need to com-municate, and you have all the *ingredients* of narrative. But how do we put them together?

From Temporal Experience to Narrative

Psychologist Daniel Stern, author of *The Present Moment in Psychotherapy and Everyday Life*, has spent years studying how people create internal nar-ratives. As part of his work, he conducted hundreds of "breakfast inter-views" in which he asked people to describe what they remembered about their breakfast routine on an ordinary morning. After asking subjects to differentiate between things they remembered and things they didn't ac-tually remember but assumed "must have happened," Stern concluded that we are unaware of much of our daily existence. Too much information streams through our bodies and minds to be able to process everything and continue to absorb new information. As we drive home from work, most of the time we are unaware of the white stripes zipping by beneath us, the flutter of birds overhead, the faint pressure of sunglasses resting on our cheeks, and a thousand other things we could notice, and could remem-ber, if we had reason to. In *Sketch of the Past*, Virginia Woolf refers to these stretches of unawareness as, "non-being . . . a kind of nondescript 'cotton wool.'"

So what stirs us to awareness? After studying the breakfast interviews, Stern concluded that what rises to awareness is the novel or unexpected, and things we perceive to be a conflict or problem. The problems that rouse us to consciousness can be extremely small. While making a morning cup of coffee yesterday, my first problem was how to turn the kettle off as soon as it began to whistle to avoid waking my family, and then, how much water to pour into the filter cup to keep it from spilling over as it had the day before, and then, whether to move the pickle jar so that I could place the milk in a more secure spot in the refrigerator. We become aware in order to consider cause and effect, take action, address the unexpected, and resolve the conflict that has roused us to consciousness.

Our considerations of problem, cause, action, and effect—whether in words, pictures, or some other form—are essentially mininarratives. When the pickle jar stuck, I flashed back to the time I broke a jam jar by yanking it off the shelf, then considered whether to cross the kitchen and look for a sponge as I glanced at the passel of papers under my purse, and then at my wristwatch, to see if I had time to deal with my kitchen conundrums before racing off to work. These daily narratives aren't particularly chronological—we slice back and forth considering multiple pasts and possible futures at terrific speed, but because we become aware of a problem or potential problem that *has arisen*, in order to take *present* action, to bring about a desired *future*, our narratives *seem* chronological.

Because the past and our expectations about the future are not subject to direct observation, we rely on communication to share and preserve our understanding of what has happened and what could happen. Through speech and writing we bring the past and future out of the realm of the "imaginary"—that is, only in our minds—and into the actual and actualized world of others. Even when we're alone, most of us think by conversing with others or an imagined duplicate self.

We continually relegate our current thoughts and actions to memory as we update sensory information and future expectations, a process that gives us the impression that we are "moving through" the present. If we didn't quickly relegate a moment ago to the past, "now" and five minutes ago would be the same "present" and we would not know where we were. As we move closer to a goal, the future appears to shrink and the past grows larger because the number of steps that we expect to take to reach a goal (or the time we've allotted to take them) decreases, and the number of steps already taken, which are now part of our past experience, increases. It is not the future that shrinks, but our perspective on how much time remains before we reach the end point that changes as we advance toward a goal or the anticipated end of life.

Plot relies upon our experience of shrinking future; a sense of shrinking future is what causes readers to grow anxious when an unexpected obstacle prevents the protagonist from proceeding toward her goal at a comfortable rate. Delay creates tension, urgency, and pressure—a sympathetic impulse within the reader that urges the protagonist to act or make the right decision as he runs out of (future) time. This explains why in story, as in life, the small glitch at the end of a process can evoke more tension than a larger obstacle encountered early on: it is the time left to fix a problem that counts.

Philosopher Martin Heidegger believed that what we care about, and how our care is manifested, is more fundamental to our sense of being-in-the-world than anything else. Putting Stern and Heidegger together, what rises to awareness depends upon what we perceive to be a problem, and what we define as a problem depends on what we care about. The nature and focus of our caring also drives what we consider to be solutions, how we solve problems, the relative priority we assign to concurrent problems, and how we measure our success. The stuck pickle jar is still in the refrigerator, but I made it to class and after class, I called my son and then sat down to revise this essay. The internal narratives people construct about ordinary moments of conflict and response reveal a great deal about their concerns and how they view themselves and the world. In other words, plot builds character, and character builds plot. And care drives both.

From Life's Clocks to Story Clock

Most lives and most great stories involve three general "frames" of temporal awareness. The human life-span is our most obvious physical and psychological time frame. But life is contingent—we never know when we are going to die—and life must be lived over years, so within the life span we continually construct sub-lifetime frames to hold and work out our life-span fears, goals, problems, and plans. Beyond the life span there are larger and longer-than-life-span generational, communal, and universal goals, fears, and themes. Of course, every larger-than-life force that an individual faces must be faced within his or her life span, and an individual life must be lived day by day. Thus larger-than-life themes in creative nonfiction are necessarily embedded in ordinary moment-to-moment events and undertakings.

Since story doesn't have a biological life span, the author must select a story's time/life span. Within that span something important must be at stake. It doesn't have to involve literal life or death, but as Eudora Welty has observed, "It does need to be a matter of spiritual or moral survival." When the writer or narrator directly or indirectly signals to the reader the microcosm of time in which the story will take place and the story's central "care" or concern, the reader feels the story's "clock" start, and consciously or subconsciously thinks, "Okay, we're rolling. This matters." She may even literally pitch forward, engaging more fully as she discerns that something important is at stake, even if she doesn't know precisely what that something is:

> On the twenty-ninth of July, in 1943, my father died. On the same day, a few hours later, his last child was born. Over a month before this, while all our energies were concentrated in waiting for these events, there had been, in Detroit, one of the bloodiest race riots of the century. A few hours after my father's funeral, while he lay in state in the undertaker's chapel, a race riot broke out in Harlem. On the morning of the third of August, we drove my father to the graveyard through a wilderness of smashed plate glass.
>
> The day of my father's funeral had also been my nineteenth birthday.

In the opening of James Baldwin's essay, *Notes of a Native Son*, the narrator clearly signals that the essay will interweave his coming-of-age and family (especially his relationship with his father), death, loss, and the violent times that his family and community inhabit. The place and time are identified—1948 and Harlem—but Baldwin also includes broader references to "the century" and "Detroit"—half a country away. The passage is full of references to time, twelve references in five sentences, and many of them have an expectant quality: "on the same day, a few hours later his last child was born," "over a month before this, while all our energies were concentrated in waiting," and "the day of my father's funeral had also been my nineteenth birthday." After reading a single paragraph the reader knows that the story span involves a young black man on the edge of adulthood, surrounded by life and death within the context of a broader and dangerous American geography.

The information that starts a story clock can be ambiguous or mysterious and still pitch us into the story.

> As a teenager Diane Arbus used to stand on the window ledge of her parents' apartment at the San Remo, eleven stories above Central Park West. She would stand there on the edge for as long as she could, gazing out at the trees and skyscrapers in the distance, until her mother pulled her back inside. Years later, Diane would say: "I wanted to see if I could do it." And she would add, "I didn't inherit my kingdom for a long time."

In the opening to Patricia Bosworth's biography of Diane Arbus, it's not completely clear what Arbus means by seeing if she could do it. Bosworth's cryptic excerpt suggests both balancing on the edge of life and death, and jumping. Nor is it clear whether Arbus's reference to "inheriting her kingdom" refers to the New York vista, or the kingdom she would gain by balancing on the narrow ledge between inside and outside, life or death, or all of these things. What is apparent is that the story will lead to significant transformative change—that a teenager still under the watchful eye of her mother will come to inherit a kingdom—and that risk and precariousness will play an ongoing role. Arbus didn't stand on the window ledge; she "used to stand"—as in, she did it often, and she stood there "as long as she could."

Instead of pitching the reader forward, Jon Krakauer's *Into Thin Air,* begins with an emotional reverse.

> Straddling the top of the world, one foot in China and the other in Nepal, I cleared the ice from my oxygen mask, hunched a shoulder against the wind, and stared absently down at the vastness of Tibet. I understood on some dim, detached level that the sweep of earth beneath my feet was a spectacular sight. I'd been fantasizing about this moment, and the release of emotion that would accompany it, for many months. But now that I was finally here, actually standing on the summit of Mount Everest, I just couldn't summon the energy to care.

Here Krakauer takes a cliché-ishly dramatic event and twists it, beginning at the end of the first sentence, with the words, "stared absently." Each succeeding sentence links strong, dramatic adjectives and verbs, such as: "spectacular," "release," "fantasizing," "hunched," and "sweep," with their emotional opposites: "dim," "detached," "absently," and "couldn't care." And in this place of great drama the narrator declares that, contrary to common sense, lack of caring wins out—which pretty much sums up the book's central puzzle.

Translating Lived Experience to the Page

In *Poetics,* our oldest surviving work of literary theory, Aristotle described the essence of *lived experience* as the movement from a beginning (concordance), through conflict and action (discordance), to resolution (a new concordance)—the same path that Daniel Stern noticed in his breakfast interviews. To transform the essence of lived experience into art, Aristotle believed that a work must have three features: completeness, wholeness, and appropriate magnitude. A work is whole if it has a (satisfying) beginning, middle, and end. The "beginning" is the last event that doesn't mandate what follows, that is, a moment of concordance before "care" recognizes a discordance, and the story emerges. The end is characterized by a return to concordance (so no further action is required) although the characters or narrator or both are changed, often radically so, for having taken the story-journey, so the end's concordance is not the same as the beginning's. The middle is defined by succession—it is compelled by (or is the consequence of) what came before, and must occur before one can reach resolution (e.g., a new concordance).

Aristotle revered stories that build to a reversal or turning point ("peripetia") accompanied by some kind of recognition ("anagnōrisis): a "kairos" moment in which the protagonist's fortune turns from good to bad (or vice versa) and, in the process, produces some larger-than-individual-life effect. In ancient Greece there were two words and gods for time—Chronos and Kairos. Chronos, the personification of clock time, was an incorporeal god with no material body or form, although sometimes he was depicted as a snake with three heads, presumably suggesting past, present, and future. Kairos was the god of the "fleeting moment," or "favorable opportunity opposing the fate of man," and personified the moment in which a man could alter his fate, or change a course of events. Such a moment could be grasped by grabbing on to the forelock that hung from Kairos's forehead, but if one did not grasp at the right instant, the moment was lost, for Kairos was bald in the back. In *The Present Moment in Psychotherapy and Everyday Life* Daniel Stern offers a contemporary definition of kairos:

> Kairos is a moment of opportunity, when events demand action or are propitious for action. Events have come together in this moment and their meeting enters awareness such that action must be taken, now, to alter one's destiny— be it for the next minute or a lifetime. If no action is taken, one's destiny will be changed anyway, but differently, because one did not act.

Virginia Woolf refers to such perception-altering moments of clarity in her unfinished memoir as "moments of being":

Week after week passed at St Ives and nothing made any dint upon me. Then, for no reason that I know about, there was a sudden violent shock; something happened so violently that I have remembered it all my life. . . . I was fighting with Thoby on the lawn. We were pommelling each other with our fists. Just as I raised my fist to hit him, I felt: why hurt another person? I dropped my hand instantly, and stood there, and let him beat me. I remember the feeling. It was a feeling of hopeless sadness. It was as if I became aware of something terrible; and of my own powerlessness.

We all have kairos moments in our lives, even if we don't recognize them until afterwards. Aristotle's discussion of reversal and recognition focuses on tragedy, but many stories not classified as "tragedy" also lead to a "kairos" moment which brings the story's dissonance into a new consonance. As poet April Barnard notes, "Our lives turn on a moment, not plot."

A work that has a beginning, middle, and end is whole, but to be complete it must have the necessary causal links to carry the action and story from the beginning through discordance and reversal to resolution. Since necessity or probability drives succession, events that do not move the story forward can be omitted. Readers do not ask what the protagonist did between two events that would have been separated in her life if a causal connection or logical progression binds the events together. In life, we also skip from event, to observation, to event based on importance and relevance, rather than chronology. When my colleague asks, "And then what happened?" she doesn't want to know that I went to the bank machine or got my haircut unless these actions propel a story forward. No one really cares about what comes next; they care about the next important thing.

In Aristotle-speak, "magnitude" is the length of time and number and kind of events needed to permit a credible change from good to bad or vice versa. A story must be long enough for a change to be believable, but not so long that readers are bogged down in unnecessary information or scenes that aren't relevant, probable, or part of the necessary succession that leads from beginning to end. We've all seen movies with fight scenes that don't advance the plot or read books in which the endings feel contrived because there wasn't sufficient development of character or event to make the resolutions seem plausible. The appropriate length or "magnitude" is the number of actions or events required for the change(s) to seem believable, and the period of time over which the necessary change takes place.

To follow a story is to understand the successive actions, thoughts, and feelings presented by the writer as they unfold with a particular "directedness" suggested by the starting of the story clock. The story's conclusion furnishes the point of view from which readers will view the tale as a whole. Thus the final statement acts as a lens through which we view the resolution of the story's central concern rather than necessarily being the last event in chronological time. In *Truly Wilde* Joan Schenkar describes Oscar Wilde's niece, Dorothy Wilde's, final, peripatetic, addicted years and death, but then circles back in the final two chapters and concludes with a love letter of unconditional acceptance that Wilde has written to Natalie Barney. By placing the letter at the end of the story, Schenkar allows us to see the protagonist as having been partially, but profoundly, victorious in her struggle with love rather than as a primarily sad or lost figure.

Looking Back to Look Forward

When a memoirist, biographer, or historian narrates events she has lived, witnessed, or "re-searched," the reader implicitly understands that the telling is a composed reconstruction. The reader also assumes that the narrator has some point or purpose (stake) in telling.

Fiction may be born from the impulse to ask—"what if ?"—but creative nonfiction has its roots in our need to understand cause and effect, to know "why?" or "how" a thing happened as we tell "what happened." As philosopher Paul Ricoeur reminds us, telling what has happened cannot be extricated from a narrator's view of why something has happened any more than it can be separated from a narrator's cares and concerns. As much as we would like to think otherwise, there are no detachable conclusions. The narrative as a whole supports the conclusions, and the conclusions are as much a product of narrative order and selection as the irrefutable facts.

In creating our internal narratives we focus on problems and solutions defined by what we care about. In creative nonfiction the narrator also decides what will be included in the story based on what she "cares about," and that is defined by the question the narrator is trying to answer, the reason the narrator is posing the question, and why the question won't go away until it's answered. From the narrator's perspective, this is why the story is being told. The narrator's inquiry follows a separate but similar trajectory to that of the tale she is telling: there is a problem, conflict, or nagging discrepancy (discordance) that focuses the narrator's attention on the story, and the narrator comes to believe that by tracking down the elements of the conflict and telling the story (taking action), she will learn something that will answer her concern and bring her (present) life into greater concordance.

Unraveling a story and then reweaving actions, thoughts, gestures, and events into a narrative that's more satisfying than the partial or puzzling explanation one started with can be a difficult and laborious process. Every retrospecting narrator is looking for a more coherent explanation because the existing internal or external narrative does not adequately explain an event or her experience. But if a writer is to see the situation in a new light, she must set aside prior judgments and configurations. One thing "because of" another is not always easy to discern from one thing "after" another, and so, for most of us, there is a good deal of flailing around in granular experience, hazy implications, and temporally complex thoughts feelings, causes, and actions. The narrator's care and concern determines what is treated as significant and what extraneous, but an organic work is also the product of a dialogue between the narrator's inquiry fueled by her care and the protagonist's actions and concerns driven by the circumstances she faces.

In Aristotle's paradigm, a work with wholeness and completeness prompts a reader to look back at the story as a whole, but not forward. Horror and pity achieved through the reversal of fortune and recognition are released in "catharsis"—a unity of feeling that encompasses the grandeur and sorrow of the human condition—as the protagonist comes to understand the larger or deeper meaning of his dilemma and his relations with himself and others. This moment of release may approximate the release from further striving that St. Augustine believed characterizes the end of life when one rejoins the ever-present eternal. However, for the living, such moments—grand though they may be—are transient, yielding to the next problem that finds its way to consciousness on the wings of care and urges us to action.

In creative nonfiction, be it memoir or history or narrative journalism, there is an implicit promise that life will go on, so the story isn't really complete in the way that drama or fiction can be complete. The creative nonfiction writer's quest may be for complete understanding, but she usually has to settle for learning—for pursuing a question defined and informed by care through the tunnels and recesses of memory, research, reflection, language, and craft in order to convey to the reader the physical, emotional, and cognitive complexity of what she has learned—knowing that it is not the last word.

Creative nonfiction's strength and challenge is that, while it can explore and dabble in closure and eternity, its ultimate allegiance is to the ongoing lived life. History and memoir may be based on the past, but the purpose of memory is to inform the present in order to positively affect the future. In addition to the complete story being told by the narrator, in the course of the telling the narrator gathers meaning from the past and thrusts it forward into the present for an unknown perilous future. As I snap off the alarm clock to begin a new day, I realize that the reason so many memoirs, histories, and other retrospectively told tales—from Joshua Wolf Shenk's *Lincoln's Melancholy* and Julia Blackburn's *The Emperor's Last Island*, to Richard Hoffman's *Half the House* and Jeanette Wall's *The Glass Castle*—close in the narrator's present, is because a teller reminds us that, while the story being told may be over, the lives on which we stake our care and stories have just begun.

JOY CASTRO

GRIP AND GETTING "GRIP"

GRIP

Over the crib in the tiny apartment, there hung a bullet-holed paper target, the size and dark shape of a man—its heart zone, head zone, perforated where my aim had torn through: thirty-six little rips, no strays, centered on spots that would make a man die.

Beginner's luck, said the guys at the shooting range, at first. *Little lady*, they'd said, until the silhouette slid back and farther back. They'd cleared their throats, fallen silent.

A bad neighborhood. An infant child. A Ruger GP .357 with speed-loader.

It's not as morbid as it sounds, a target pinned above a crib: the place was small, the walls already plastered full with paintings, sketches, pretty leaves, hand-illuminated psychedelic broadsides of poems by my friends. I masking-taped my paper massacre to the only empty space, a door I'd closed to form a wall.

When my stepfather got out of prison, he tracked my mother down. He found the city where she'd moved. He broke a basement window and crawled in. She never saw his car, halfway up the dark block, stuffed behind a bush.

My mother lived. She wouldn't say what happened in the house that night. Cops came: that's what I know. Silent, she hung a screen between that scene and me. It's what a mother does.

She lived—as lived the violence of our years with him, knifed into us like scrimshaw cut in living bone.

Carved but alive, we learned to hold our breath, dive deep, bare our teeth to what fed us.

When I was twenty-one, my son slept under the outline of what I could do, a death I could hold in my hands.

At the time, I'd have denied its locale any meaning, called its placement coincidence, pointing to walls crowded with other kinds of dreams.

But that dark, torn thing did hang there, its lower edge obscured behind the wooden slats, the flannel duck, the stuffed white bear.

It hung there like a promise, like a headboard, like a *No,* like a terrible poem, like these lines I will never show you, shielding you from the fear I carry—like a sort of oath I swore over your quiet sleep.

GETTING "GRIP"

When I finished my memoir *The Truth Book,* I thought I was done with life-writing. I looked forward to returning to fiction and poetry, the genres in which I had trained. *The Truth Book* was harrowing to draft, harrowing to revise—even harrowing to read from when I toured: I would return to my hotel rooms exhausted and febrile, trembling, drinking Airborne like a toddy in town after town. When the book's launch was over, I felt relief. I'd gone public with all that awful old material I'd secretly carried (child abuse, fundamentalism, adoption, confusion about my *latinidad,* prison, suicide), and I could let it rest.

I was done drawing on my life for material. *Good-bye to all that.*

So "Grip" came as a surprise.

Genre

"Grip" came as a poem, initially—a free-verse poem all in one long stanza that obsessed over its central remembered image: the dark, torn paper target hanging over the baby's sweet crib, the contrast of which struck me as strange and compelling in a way it had not when I'd hung the target there myself many years and many dwellings ago.

I can't remember now whether I originally wrote the poem longhand—which is likely, because that's how I draft almost everything, including this essay—or on my computer in my office, which is where I tinkered with the piece between classes and committee meetings, reading it aloud to myself, gradually seeing that it wanted to break into stanzas. White space helped mark the temporal and topical shifts.

Eventually, the lineation seemed to want to fall away. As a reader, I always wonder if a free-verse poem needs to be a poem. Sometimes the line breaks do seem important, but sometimes they don't. In the case of "Grip," they didn't. So I let them go, and the piece melted into paragraphs that were indented where the stanzas had begun.

"Grip" came to make more aesthetic sense to me as a very short essay that cares a lot about sound—repetition, rhythm, rhyme—than as a poem.

Audience

I am usually very unsure about my work—about whether the material that surprises or moves me will matter to anyone else—and it was so with this essay, too.

During the time I was composing it, I was obliged to give a reading every six months at the Pine Manor College MFA program, where I teach. Since most of the faculty and students are there each time, you always have to read something new (or else look washed up). I tried "Grip" out on the audience, and they were very enthusiastic. I was lucky: the audience included poet and editor Steven Hul, who later read "Grip" aloud on his radio show; and the poets Meg Kearney and Laure-Anne Bosselaar, who said kind things about it; and Mike Steinberg, a founding editor of *Fourth Genre*.

Their enthusiastic reception encouraged me to try submitting it. The audience can be very important. It's such a reciprocal relationship.

My real audience, though, is young mothers from backgrounds of poverty and violence, women desperate like the woman I was. I hope "Grip" reaches them.

POV

One writerly rule of thumb is not to switch POV in tight quarters, so I worried over the last section of "Grip," which opens by talking about "my son" in the third person, but then pulls a swerve at the very end and speaks directly to him: "like these lines I will never show you, shielding you from the fear I carry—like a sort of oath I swore over your quiet sleep." The whole thing, I hope the reader can see at that point, has been addressed to him all along— but won't be disclosed to him. To know the pain and intensity your parents carry is too heavy a burden.

That's what I believed when I composed it, anyway. When I learned it was going to be on the air and might eventually be published, I worried. We'd had a bad moment a couple of years before, when a high school friend had told him something from *The Truth Book*. He had decided earlier not to read it, knowing from the subtitle (*Escaping a Childhood of Abuse among Jehovah's Witnesses*) that it would make him sad. I thought that was a healthy boundary for him to draw.

But then his friend read the book and asked him about something. When he came home, he cried. "Did that happen to you?" he said. It really hurt him.

I didn't want to put him through anything similar again, so I gave him a copy of "Grip" to read, and by then, he was older and in college and thought it was a good idea to do so. When he read it, he was pretty unfazed. Kids will surprise you.

The POV switch had troubled me from a technical standpoint, so I tried a number of alternatives to make the piece more consistent; but nothing else felt true. I gave up temporarily, and when I read the piece aloud at Pine Manor with the POV switch intact, it didn't seem to baffle or bother anyone. I left it alone after that.

Submerged

When I submitted "Grip" to *Fourth Genre*, it did not include paragraphs six through eight ("My mother lived . . ."). There was a leap, a gap, and it sounded almost as though my mother could have been dead. She wasn't, but I sort of liked the drama and the absence of certainty.

The editor at *Fourth Genre*, Marcia Aldrich, suggested some changes: "The unanswered question as to your mother's fate is troubling, and a bit more on the roots of the fear that motivates the need to protect your son was identified in our readers' reports. Speaking for myself, I wanted a bit more grounding, or a slight nod in that direction." This seemed like a simple request for fair play with the reader, so I expanded the essay to address those concerns. I added the clarifying material: my mother lived. I agreed with the request for changes, which made it a stronger, fuller piece.

However, I wanted to make sure the essay still said that you could survive something and yet not be alive in quite the same way you were before. To convey something about the way violence can catalyze a kind of poetry of action—not does, *can*—I got the idea of "scrimshaw cut in living bone," which expressed, I thought, an untenable violation that nonetheless might produce a desperate sort of beauty (like hanging a target over a crib). Then I got carried away with literalizing the scrimshaw notion and felt obliged to include the whole whale—an actual whale, swimming about the paragraph. I ran a revised version past my friend and colleague James Engelhardt, a poet and the managing editor at *Prairie Schooner*, who kindly suggested that my inclusion might be a bit over the top, and he was right. It was too abrupt: the reader is first in my old apartment and then at the shooting range, and then sees my mother get attacked, only to be dragged to the depths by a whale that's only metaphorical anyway. Ugh.

So I cut the whale but kept the scrimshaw line, which was all I'd really wanted, and a couple of other phrases that were salvageable: "we learned to hold our breath, dive deep, bare our teeth to what fed us."

In this way, the whale is there, yet not there, and posterity will be relieved to find no krill in the piece.

Synecdoche

My stepfather's sexual abuse of me has caused long-lasting damage, but I didn't want to go into all that in "Grip." I'd hashed through it in *The Truth Book*, and I thought that bringing such an explosive topic into so short an essay could derail the piece.

But while I tried to squelch it, it was there for me, psychically, as I was writing. I kept telling it, *This isn't about you: it's about my mom, and my son*, but it wouldn't let itself be silenced. So I compromised with it: I looked for a concrete, true detail that would let me allude to it, which I found in this image of the target: "But that dark, torn thing did hang there, its lower edge obscured behind the wooden slats, the flannel duck, the stuffed white bear."

That hidden lower edge of the outline—hidden behind the crib slats, hidden in the essay—stood in for my stepfather's abusive sexuality. It functioned as a synecdoche for all of it.

My psyche accepted that line as a reasonable compromise, a sufficient acknowledgment of that issue, and left me in peace.

The reader doesn't need to know.

Title

The title "Grip" was simply a gift. It just came, early on, very soon after the initial poem was down on the page, and although it isn't a word that occurs in the body of the text, it seemed right: my grip on the gun, the grip of fear, trying to keep a grip on yourself, the urgent but futile project of gripping your children to keep them safe. For me as a writer, it even referred to my grip on this particular material, which always felt a little tenuous.

"Grip": short, apt, evocative, and easy to recall. I kept questioning and testing its rightness throughout the revision process, but it stuck.

Form

In form, I prefer short over long, the slap to the lecture.

This preference may come from being raised to be seen and not heard, raised as a girl in what was then a very male-dominated religion. Women were exhorted to be silent, and my family echoed that precept and enforced it with violence. In such a context, if you open your mouth, you'd better have something important to say.

Of course, I don't agree with that now, but it was my world from birth to fourteen, and it had its effect on my aesthetic. Although I've been a professor for twelve years, the lectern remains an uneasy space for me (even though I now say things like "space"). Holding forth: very difficult. The sound of my own voice in public for any stretch of time makes me nervous, and it's that way on the page, too.

Also, I get bored easily, and I resent writers who bore me, so I don't want to bore anyone else.

Short works for me. Compression. Urgency. Get in, get out.

It's funny to me that this essay is longer than "Grip" itself.

Patience

I always encourage students to let things lie. Let them settle. When you're going through the thick of something—whether you're breaking up your marriage or climbing Mount Kilimanjaro—it's hard to do anything except journalism. Take notes, sure. But don't try to force art from it. It's too close. You can't see it yet.

The patterns—the ones that really illuminate, reveal, show something new—don't emerge that quickly. They can take years to surface from the welter of immediate detail.

I was twenty-one when I hung that bullet-holed target over my son's crib, and it didn't strike me as macabre or even as a possible strange form of oath until my very late thirties, when I suddenly saw it: saw that dark target hanging there over the crib in my mind's eye and thought, for the first time, *Hey, that's weird. What was I thinking?* I saw it in conjunction with the fear I'd carried and my mother's attack by her abusive husband long after she'd left him, moved to another state, and believed herself safe. I could see her failure to protect my brother and me juxtaposed starkly against that black gun in my hands. But at twenty-one, I couldn't have told you any of that.

My son, as I write this, will be twenty-one himself in October. A lot of time has passed since the events "Grip" narrates.

What I'm saying is that it takes time to see. You have to acquire a different perspective to see your old self anew, to see the patterns that have been lying there all along. That's what creative nonfiction is about for me.

Be patient. Don't rush your work; don't force it. Keep writing and reading while you wait.

I've been helped by teaching and studying literature from an analytical, scholarly standpoint. When I'm teaching a story by Daniel Chacón or a poem by Elizabeth Bishop, I have to approach it in a cool, neutral way to see how its parts work to make meaning, and how the writer is re-creating a world in language. Doing that constantly, for a living, could kill the creative impulse outright, and I worry about that, but in the meantime, it has schooled me to a kind of alertness about language and effect. If you're a professor, there's a danger of your work becoming professorial: too suffused by the living death of committee meetings and the unacknowledged privilege of having the leisure to pick over small things at great length. But if you can manage to avoid that, analyzing a lot of literature can be a good way to build your tool kit.

Keep training. Keep gaining skills. Write sonnets and haiku and villanelles—write a novel!—so that you have multiple techniques at your fingertips. Then, when something about your experience does strike you as genuinely provocative or strange, you'll be able to bring it full-force to the page.

ADVICE AND ON WRITING "ADVICE"

ADVICE

Dear,

Why do some men wear such tight pants, and why are they getting tighter these days?

My Friend,

Men wear tight pants because their legs—thighs, calves, ankles—have been long overlooked. Note the poor ankle, stripped bare by socks rubbing. Today's trends, or being in a band, serve up an excuse for tight jeans, black, or dark blue, so men might show off a thigh's curve. But more than this, men who would slip into the body of a woman let their pants suggest this, whisper it, the stiff fabric hauled up over hips, which, too, have gone unremarked, slim hips, slight as a girl's. Such a man minds not at all the mocking of his father, wants no handy loop for the hammer, doesn't care to be handy (for this is about legs and not hands), his jeans so tight his friends laugh and say *nice junk, package, stash, man.* So when he sits, there's a fold, a pressure, slight ache at the crease to remind him.

Walking at dusk, the shadow he is passes over benches and curbs, narrows, resembles that of a woman, and again it's that time, years ago now, when he turned sideways and was called by a girl's name, was mistaken for her and he played along—so well, in fact, that it felt not at all like a mistake. He stages now, for himself, double takes late mornings in gardens, slant against buildings at the end of the day. He returns her, there she is, so he's not so alone, she comes back, the steep dark of another, and *he,* scissory, loose-hinged, at home in the ease and expanse of his body, is *she*. No wind billows his cuffs (no cuffs at all, rolled or bunched, fraying, workerish, *these* jeans are skinny as pencils). What is she whispering, so close to him now as he rests on a stoop, bends his knees, makes a lap, brief ambient space for a dog, for a child . . . ? My Friend, they wear their pants tight so as to feel *she's here again.* To quietly, secretly, call her back in.

Dear,

How can I roll around more in nuance and say the fineness of what comes to me, hovering, wordless, what we know to call *thinking*? So often the edges of thought get sheared, tints hardily brightened, rambles clear-cut. The time I need to meander gets claimed, touched, obligated. Then it's tainted. And I'm left with bald statements and gist.

My Friend,

I have a story I want to tell you.

And here, I almost said, "When I learned to shoot . . ." in order to talk about nuance, that fragile state you describe. It was something about holding the stock tight to my shoulder, the surprise taste of oil when I snuck a lick off the barrel—but in bringing the moment into the light, to you, to our readers, a formalness came. I mean, it took form, found a shape much too quickly. "When I learned to shoot . . ." seemed, for a moment, orderly and right as an introduction. But I've shot a gun only twice. The first time, into a blue sky at clay pigeons and my aim was very badly off, and the second on a farm in Poland at cans on a fence, where I hit every one. That was great, but to say "when I learned to shoot" suggests I've kept up—and I haven't.

I have to reorient now, slow down and figure out how to link up your question (I know you struggled to put it together) with my thought—hardly formed, full of promise—about shooting, the taste of gun oil, scrollwork on the stock I ran my nail over, crescent of dirt I scraped from the barrel, sun in the scope, calm of the scope's much-narrowed world, the space there contained, the order and peace unbidden and also unnerving. I'll have to get back to that scattery inkling, or try to shape it anew, either way, overturn that force driving toward statement, toward fixing a point, the point overtaking and bent on sealing up thought . . . and well, yes, that takes *time*. I see what you mean—about the circling and hovering, and how hard it is to get the world to allow it. How difficult to clear space for a ramble. To love time. To get time to love you.

I'll try again. A different route now.

Leaving Chicago a few weeks ago, I saw from the window of the plane, a wall in Lake Michigan. It was parallel to the shore, I couldn't tell how far out—a knuckle's length from so far up, as I closed one eye and measured. It looked like an Etch A Sketch line, stylus-drawn through a silver emulsion. A boat was motoring from shore toward the wall, leaving behind a white wave that dissolved. It was hard to judge speed, but it seemed the boat wanted to sidle up very close, wanted to fold itself into the concrete. As in the airport just this morning, the woman with the prosthetic leg (leg and hip, judging by stiffness) whose skirt was worn through with three little holes where the contraption rubbed, returned to me that sensation of awkward rotation-and-pivot. In the year I wore a body cast, I, too, rubbed holes in the backs of shirts where I leaned against walls and lockers and cars. Small, precise holes where my cast was rough. Seeing that woman, I knew again (anyone might, this isn't clairvoyance) what it was like to be kept far from the bodies of others. *"Those little holes."* I said it only to myself. I didn't speak the words aloud (nuance needs space to hover and *roll around* as you note) because how would that sound to her: *I know about the holes. Those are my holes.* So close were the holes all these years! Who knew I'd enter them again, that I'd kept them for just this moment so I might seal up the distance between my body and hers.

My Friend, such moments *do* survive. Give them air. Let them play unsupervised in the field of the body. Keep the tasks of the day aside for as long as you can. Feed silence. Invite time. Resist gist.

Dear,

The other day I wanted to give my body away. Why? I'm not, as they used to say, a "loose woman."

My Friend,

Wasn't it you who wrote a short time ago saying you felt not at all in possession of your body? But that it wasn't death, either, you meant, nor was it another form of detachment or dissociation. And when you were sitting beside a man whose grand loss was known to all, that worst of all losses, a whole family gone instantly, tragically taken . . . wasn't it then that your own surface slid? And you found no reason to dig into why, or interpret, pathologize, justify. You just wanted to give. I read in the paper the other day (yes, the very same paper that runs this column) a strange, then very right-seeming thing. These people who'd been volunteering at a local soup kitchen for seventeen years said, "We almost don't know why we come here, we've been coming here so long . . ." They call the hungry men "Sir" and the women "Ma'am." They serve up big portions, set places, clear tables, and scrub out the pots. They are not full of pity. Or no longer are. It's just easy, habitual giving and doing.

Wouldn't you want it be, to him, a relief? Wasn't it that your body, just then, needed not one single thing? Only to give, to offer itself. After much generosity of the daily kind (small things matter, too: take in mail for the neighbors, water plants, listen well), your body meant to extend itself *further*. Into. Another. Be *for* another. This is, after all, an advice column. Who writes and asks who hasn't lost something, or isn't afraid of losses to come, or is presently losing and lacks the will to believe it?

Once I sat next to a man on a train whose back didn't work well—it must have been fused, it stayed rigid as he rose from his seat—and he looked to be in great pain. He held his side with one hand and his head with the other; he rested his head against the train window to redistribute the weight and the pressure, but his breath was still fitful. He stretched a little, as much as he could, then angled stiffly back into his seat where he sighed very deeply. And of that relief, I knew this: it's momentary. All that positioning for a moment of respite.

A dose of respite so the wincing would stop, so the loss would cease, is what *you'd* be, right, for the man you just wrote of? A place to lean into and breathe—your hair, if it's long, or your neck with its oceany warmth, scent of grass because we're all going (*really going,* or wanting to go sooner because of the pain), that bit of relief, so pain in its constancy might be put off, its edges worn softer—you'd *be* that. You'd get to be part of the moment, the site at which even a brief ease asserted.

Yes, Friend, it's criminal to hold back, stay apart, when one might give and give and give. But we've set this up for the greater good. For the worth of other intactnesses, for the sake of family and order, and country, the body is barred from some forms of giving. For all the body learns to bar, *Amen,* we learn to say.

So you're useless, beautiful body behaves. You stay still—as anyone might—in the shivery, mutinous light of loss. Light in gimcracks through fall's granite clouds. Light sliding along the bent ribs of pumpkins. Loss translucing the sugar from maples, the tender backlit leaves aflare. Light rashing us all, slow, fretted and grand. Friend, it's hard to imagine the body in pain when it isn't. Or when you're sweating on a subway in August, hard to conjure the distant and soundless cold mornings of winter.

I believe our best work on earth is in service of likeness. I don't know what to call it—moments of interpenetration? To feel the exchange across borders. You're writing, I think, to say how much you want to work for such a cause. Readers, a challenge: hear past your associations with the word *penetrate*; break it down, past the brutish, go back to its origins: "to place within, to enter within, related to *penitus*: interior, in-most, the in-most recesses." To enter, to be entered is a beautiful thing. Though, yes, how hard to contain complications when bodies are involved. Thanks, Friend, for writing.

Dear,

I'm writing again. I'm not finished, though your answer was good. You're right. It is hard. Why is it so especially hard to convince others I'd want nothing in return for the body's work? Enough to be the passage through which alleviation moves. Which feels ancient, and clean, like the form of a simple canoe, mano, plinth. Or a very brief poem, a fragment, a moment so full it needs no expounding—Heraclitus' "the harmony past knowing / sounds more deeply than the known" for example.

My Friend,

Perhaps we should consider the aqueducts of Rome for a moment. These days, in Romavecchia, a suburb just north of the city, runners use the precisely spaced arches to mark distance, dogs piss against them, kids slouch and kiss and smoke under the yellowing stone. In the past, in their time, aqueducts filled the baths, fountains, public drinking spouts of Rome, watered terraces, flushed the entire city's sewer system—ah, to make with the body such a system of response, a tonic, balm, respite! (Heraclitus back at you—"Silence, healing.") My Friend, it's a structural question you're asking. How a thing stands up to time, adapts, changes. Shows itself to be a passage, and useful, anew.

Perhaps we are too fixed in our bodies.

This might help:

Once I saw in a new, slick hotel a very mod bathtub with high sides like a big teacup. Anyone would look fragile in it, unformed and diminished by its size. I imagined at rest there many wet bodies, each as tender as the underside of a wrist, that patch where life could be so easily let. In the low light, it suggested the soft milks of Vermeer, cream in the unspiraling peel of the lemon, the lilac and sulfur hanging in air, gembright wine in cut roemers blackening, mossy greens pocking the cut wheels of cheese, puckering apples, freshly killed pheasant rainbowing dark corners—in decline, such brimming; in quietude, torsion.

My Friend, in order to contain the event you're discussing—the tending-after, and after, not-wanting—we would have to be different. Wider and broader. And our language would, too. Need and its overtones—desire, ownership, envy—would not be discordant. We'd carry "aftermath" easily with us, lilacs and sulfur shading the scene, the knowledge of clabbering coming on, the turning and souring under our noses, but not yet, not just yet.

If people are happiest when they're useful, then why can't the body be used for good, or lent out as needed, given over, since we're here for such a very short while? Hard question.

Dear,

I know others have questions, practical ones, about love and taxes and families and work. Just one more then. I'm sure it's related. Why is it so hard to believe that, as seen from a plane, clouds really can't hold us? I know, because they look thick and solid, they constitute a way of thinking, perpetuate childish thoughts about heaven. Still, it's hard to imagine they won't soften a fall. Such backlit white curves, such pearled, gray-bright heft . . . until your plane cuts right through, and they resist not at all. They just allow passage.

Why are they so unmoved by our passing?

ON WRITING "ADVICE"

"Advice" was a surprise in all ways.

Very soon after the initial launch (that pretty random triggering thought "why do men wear such tight pants these days"—the sort of daily musing that usually just floats in and floats off) the essay's path established: its voice split, and the thinking took on a question/response form. There are infinite ways to reason, wrangle, propose, discover in an essay. This form—a dialogue between a questioner and an advice columnist—allowed me to inhabit my own thinking in a conversational way. The questions aren't simple ones and the answers aren't definitive; the responses, in fact, are more companionate than authoritative.

Rather than advise anyone to "try writing an advice column" (that kind of mimicry is usually reductive) I'd suggest that one stay open and alert to the surprising shapes thinking takes, for maximum surprise.

SEAN PRENTISS

ETERNAL SUNSHINE OF THE NONFICTION MIND: A NEW PHILOSOPHY FOR UNDERSTANDING TRUTH AND CREATIVE NONFICTION

Growing older makes it harder to remember.
—The Hold Steady

Breaking Up with Joanne: My Version

A few years ago, my friend Jon and I share beers and talk about love and dating and arguments and breaking up. I tell him a story I have held close to my heart for fifteen years, a story of first heartbreak:

It is 1990. Early autumn. I am a freshman at East Stroudsburg University in Pennsylvania. Joanne, the girl I've dated for two years, is a high school senior and, come spring, will be crowned homecoming queen. I won't be on the football field as she is crowned because, by then, so many things will have gone sour—her taking someone else to the dance, our constant bickering across phone lines. And all that begins now, in early autumn, as Joanne and I talk over the phone. There is exhaustion in her voice as she breaks up with me.

In the weeks that follow, I learn about funneling beers, Mad Dog fortified wine, empty vodka bottles, the slow burn of pot in my lungs. And I learn to hold onto the memories of Joanne breaking up with me because that is all I have. Just memories.

The Problem:
The Broken Contract between Writer and Reader

Being a creative nonfiction (CNF) writer and professor, I am often challenged about CNF by my poet and novelist friends. They ask, "Do you really think CNF is based in truth?" I can't even answer that question because I wonder what truth they are talking about—Truth, truth, fact, or emotional truth? I do know that I often wonder about truth as I am reading a memoir that is layered in details from the writer's childhood. How can they remember all of that exactness—the meal they ate twenty years ago, the way the sun set.

My friends say, "When I read memoirs, I feel that I'm not reading the truth, that I'm being lied to." I nod my head, though calling it a lie seems a bit harsh. They ask, as they hold up a memoir, "I'm supposed to believe this is all real, right?"

These questions about whether or not CNF is delivering the truth are reasonable questions, since many CNF textbooks have "true" or "truth" in the title (*Writing True* by Sondra Perl and Mimi Schwartz, *Contemporary Creative Nonfiction: The Art of Truth* by Bill Roorbach, *The Truth of the Matter* by Dinty W. Moore, and *To Tell the Truth* by Connie D. Griffin). Other CNF textbooks discuss fact, truth, and/or emotional truth, as can be seen when Barbara Lounsberry, in *The Literature of Reality*, talks about truth being stranger than fiction or when Bruce Dobler, associate professor of English in the CNF Program at the University of Pittsburgh, says that nonfiction is "known as . . . the 'literature of fact.'" In *Keep it Real*, Lee Gutkind writes, "Creative nonfiction also explicitly engages the concept of the truth, both emotionally and literally."

These word choices, standard for CNF, lead readers and writers to believe that the genre mirrors back true events and that the contract between reader and writer calls for truthful (factually and emotionally) narratives. But the more I write and teach CNF, the more I wonder if this is the contract we should be making between writer and reader.

With these questions about CNF rattling around in my mind, I walk my Michigan neighborhood in the snow and ask my own questions of my genre.

Am I writing the truth,[1] the Truth,[2] emotional truth,[3] or fact?[4] As I pass the small bakery near my house, I wonder if I'm lying to, manipulating, or misleading the reader. As I reach the coffee shop where I plan to write, I wonder what (and where) truth is in my CNF. And I wonder what (and where) the art is.

After thinking about these questions on many walks like this one, I have come to believe that readers and writers of CNF have been taught to expect the wrong thing from our genre. Readers expect truth in our writing. But truth is an impossibility in CNF almost any way you define it.

Definitions: Getting to the Greek (and Latin) of It

Before we critique CNF's assumed contract concerning truth, we should define some terms so we can understand what they (and the genre) are and are not and how they connect to truth.

Memoir comes from the Latin word *memoria,* meaning "memory," and is a sharing of the writer's memories. Gore Vidal talks about the difference between memoir and autobiography: "A memoir is how one remembers one's own life, while an autobiography is history, requiring research, dates, facts double-checked." Vidal clearly delineates memoir from autobiography through the use of memory versus facts and history.

Essay comes from the Latin word *exagium* (through the French word *essai*), meaning "a weighing" or "to examine" or "to try." An essay, therefore, calls for an examination or the trying on of an issue or event.

CNF is harder to define since it is, by definition, based around what it is not. Maybe a good working definition is that CNF is not fiction but, like fiction, uses creative and imaginative elements to write about real people,

---

1. Which comes from the West Saxon word *triewe* and means "faithful" or having the "quality of being true."

2. Which relates to the universalist idea that there are universal facts that are unwavering.

3. How an individual feels about an event, how an event felt, or the emotional state felt during an event.

4. Is something known to be true, the universalistic truth.

places, and events. Kim Barnes calls it imposing "a narrative of meaning that represents our individual emotional truths."

Not one of these definitions mentions truth as a primary element of the genre. And there is a good reason for that. Truth is not obtainable in CNF; it is only imaginable.

Memory: The Imaginative Albums of Our Mind

Why is truth not obtainable? The major reason is that as CNF writers search for truth, we focus on probing memories for the realest and most authentic memory. The idea is that when I think about Joanne breaking up with me, if I reflect hard enough, if I take myself back to that moment on the phone and the pain I felt afterwards, I can remember the absolute truth as it occurred. And if I forget something, all I need to do is think longer and harder, to return to East Stroudsburg in my mind—see the yellowing leaves, the brick buildings, the thin clouds, the girls laughing on the quad, the emptying bottle of vodka in my fingers.

The reason we CNF writers probe our memories is because we feel that we put memories into our brains in the same way we arrange photos into photo albums. Then later, as we write, we can search for specific memories (photos) in our minds (photo albums). We expect that the memories brought forth from the album of our mind will be snippets of the original and perfect memories of an event. This is not remotely the case (though many readers and writers of CNF often believe it is, which is a big reason why readers and writers expect truth).

Joe LeDoux, the Henry and Lucy Moses Professor of Science at NYU's Center for Neural Science and the director of the Center for the Neuroscience of Fear and Anxiety, examined the theory that once a memory is created within the brain it is impossible to remove or alter because the memory is a physical part of the brain. LeDoux found that this not how memory works.

In 2000, LeDoux took a "single, specific memory [and] wiped [it] from the brains of rats" during experiments that were eerily similar to the memory-erasing techniques from the movie *Eternal Sunshine of the Spotless Mind*. LeDoux said, "The film . . . described exactly what we were doing. . . . We were zapping [memory] with a chemical, a shot of anisomycin; they zapped [memory] with a machine." The scientists chose rats because "our brains . . . work the same way" as rats' brains.

What these experiments showed was that there is a single "original" memory created at the time of an event (say the memory of Joanne and I breaking up), but this original memory is not permanently stored. Rather, the memory is re-created every time a person thinks of a remembered event. The original memory (Memory 1A) is replaced by a revised second remembering (Memory 1B) and that memory is replaced by a new remembering (Memory 1C). This re-remembering continues for as long as a person thinks of a specific memory, and each memory (1A, 1B, 1C) is different in major and minor ways. I think of all the nights I've thought about Joanne breaking up with me. What version of that memory am I on?

Besides just re-creating memory, LeDoux writes that the mind "mak[es] sense of" memory "by telling a story" and this "making sense" further moves our memories from the original event. Or as Karim Nader, an associate professor who studies memory at McGill University, says, "When you are remembering something, the memory is unstable. It's being rebuilt, re-created."

All of the above theories make memory highly unreliable if we are after the original truth of an event. If we want truth to spring from memory, we're bound to fail because, according to Abumrad and Krulwich, "there is no such thing as a memory for all times," there's just "the most recent recollection." And "the more you remember something . . . the less accurate [the memory] becomes. The more [the memory] becomes about you and the less it becomes about the act," meaning that we sculpt our memories to fit our created stories.

Abumrad and Krulwich discuss an imagined couple who shares a first kiss. As they grow old and individually think about the memory of that kiss, "the kiss will . . . become replaced by two independently re-embroidered and increasingly dishonest kisses." The original and most true memory of the first kiss (Memory 1A) vanished the moment their lips broke apart. All that remains are two creative reinterpretations (his Memory 1Z and her Memory 1Z) of that first kiss. If I had known this back in 1990, I would have wondered if and how I was re-creating the memory of my breakup with Joanne.

The Forgetting Curve: Love It or Lose It

All this research on the creativity and malleability of memory and its disconnection from the truth of an event leads to what seems like common sense—that the way to best preserve a memory would be to think about it less since the more we remember a memory the more manipulated that memory becomes. Unfortunately, the forgetting curve, discovered in 1885 by the German philosopher Hermann Ebbinghaus, highlights the speed at which memories break down.

Research shows that "humans tend to halve their memory of newly learned knowledge in a matter of days or weeks unless they consciously review the learned material." Further, according to the Counseling Services of Waterloo University, "if you have done nothing with the information you learned . . . , didn't think about it again . . . you will have lost 50%–80% of what you learned" in a matter of weeks. This loss of memory occurs because our brains take in so much information that they purge all they interpret as unneeded.

So now, as CNF writers, we're stuck between: (1) not wanting to remember too often because the act of remembering re-creates memory and (2) needing to remember as a way to slow the forgetting curve. The seemingly good news is that vivid or traumatic memories (like being broken up with by Joanne) have the slowest forgetting curve, but . . .

Eyewitness Accounts: Barely Better Than a Guess

These vivid and traumatic memories are gravely flawed because study after study shows that eyewitness accounts (around which much of CNF is based) are unreliable. According to *Truth in Justice*, eyewitness accounts used in court are wrong more than 50 percent of the time. Added to that, the Innocence Project states that almost 80 percent of exonerations based on DNA contradicted faulty eyewitness accounts. And, according to Edwin Colfax, director for the Justice Project, "Eyewitness ID reform is the No. 1 priority of people who want to reduce . . . wrongful convictions."

There is the account of Jennifer Thompson-Cannino, a college student who was raped. During the thirty-minute rape, Thompson-Cannino studied the rapist. Thompson-Cannino later said, "I tried to pay attention to the details of his face. I tried to figure out how tall he was and how much he weighed and how he put his hands on his hips and if he was pigeon-toed." Unfortunately, her testimony put the wrong man behind bars. Thompson-Cannino went on to say, "I was able to look at my attacker for [thirty minutes] at close range and I still made a mistake."

A study done by Dr. Charles Morgan III, associate professor of psychiatry at Yale University School of Medicine, adds scientific proof that eyewitnesses lose the ability to pick out subjects in stressful situations. Dr. Morgan's study offers these statistics about eyewitnesses: only "30 percent accuracy in the live line-up, 38 percent accuracy in the photo spread and 49 percent accuracy in the series of photos." Dr. Morgan's study concluded that under stressful conditions, people are unable to remember not just if an attacker is pigeon-toed but also major details like his hair color or height. Even in less stressful situations (like my breakup with Joanne), those tested were only able to correctly pick out subjects from lineups 60 percent of the time. Elizabeth Loftus, a psychologist at the University of California at Irvine who studied eyewitnesses, says that "memory may seem vivid but is often inaccurate and distorted."

So if memoir does spring from our memories, we should not expect truth because we writers would be wrong about 50 percent of the time about the big things they're remembering—how a car accident occurred or how our parents woke us to tell us of a friend's death—and 40 percent of the time with the smaller things—the meal we ate last week or, for heaven's sake, fifteen years ago.

What Now? A New Philosophy

The three memory-based issues mentioned above, (1) the re-creating of memory, (2) the forgetting curve, and (3) the flaws of eyewitnesses, serve as roadblocks to writing CNF from memory in a hope of achieving truth. These three memory-based issues make what J. A. Cuddon, author of *Dictionary of Literary Terms*, writes even more powerful: "[CNF] may be largely fictional. Few can recall clear details of their early life." So what do we do with CNF? Do we see our genre as a flawed and, therefore, useless genre because it cannot obtain truth through memory?

No.

Rather, we writers should use every resource available to work toward telling the truth in our essays and memoirs by probing memories and by doing research (looking at photographs, doing interviews, reading news accounts). But we also need to search for a new philosophy to explain CNF, a philosophy that moves writers and readers away from considering our craft's goal to be a sharing of an absolute truth, which memories cannot provide.

Immanuel Kant: If a Tree Falls in the Forest
We Each See It Differently

Immanuel Kant (1724–1804), in response to the empiricists[5] and rational-
ists,[6] came up with a system of thought called transcendental idealism, which
claimed that there were two worlds: the noumenal and the phenomenonal.
The noumenal (originating from the term *Ding an sich* and translated as
"thing-in-itself") is the actual world. The phenomenonal (anything observable) is the world of appearances.

Kant believed humans could not access the noumenal world because we
use our senses (sight, smell, touch, taste, hearing), which alters the realness
of the noumenal world. So any knowledge humans obtain comes not from
the real world (the noumenal) but from our filtered perceptions of realness
(the phenomenal). The knowledge we obtain is merely the world "as we see it"
versus the world "as it is." Broken down into mathematical terms, noumenal
truth + our senses = an individual's phenomenal truths.

To tie this idea to memories and eyewitnesses, Kant might say we should
never expect our memories (or our memoirs) to be true since we experience
life through the filter of our senses, which distorts how we remember an
event. So if CNF writers hope to tell an absolutely true story, we need to
tell the noumenal truth, but this truth, which maybe we could call Truth, is
inaccessible to humanity because, well, we are human.

Another way to explain this is that there are countless phenomenal truths
for every event. Two people (or one person at two different times) will always
remember the event differently, and at times, very differently. Details big
and small get lost, changed, or added because of the phenomenal nature of
the human experience and the imaginative nature of memory. And this all
is a beautiful thing because if we all shared noumenal truths, there'd be no

---

5. In the seventeenth and eighteenth centuries, the empiricist philosophers posited that the
mind was a blank slate, and on this blank slate the external world was etched. This etching became an exact replication of the real world. So, according to empiricists, our minds recorded the
world as it actually was, therefore, we knew and experienced the real world.

6. The rationalist philosophers of the seventeenth and eighteenth centuries posited that absolute truths were not inscribed on the mind. Rather the only way to access absolute truths was
through deductive thought alone.

need to tell stories and there would be nothing to learn about humans or the condition we live in. Instead, our phenomenal truths—unique to each individual at each moment in time—are what make us human and make our CNF narratives needed.

Myth versus Truth: The Myth of Our Truths

Another way to approach this issue is to define myth and mythology to help rethink the terms we use to describe CNF. This rethinking may move people away from the idea that CNF can or should be about noumenal truth. And it will remind readers and writers that CNF is the art of crafting shifting memories.

The definitions of a myth or mythology are these: "A traditional story accepted as history . . . to explain the worldview of a people." Or "A sacred story [that] implies neither the truth nor the falseness of the narrative. To the source culture, however, a myth by definition is 'true,' in that it embodies beliefs, concepts, and ways of questioning and making sense of the world." Or a "story . . . rooted in universal human experiences that people want to re-experience in new forms again. . . . [S]tories that are 'more than true.'"

Euhemerus, a Greek mythographer, in *Sacred History* called myths "accounts of actual historical events, distorted over many retellings," while writer, philologist, and religious thinker J. R. R. Tolkien said, "Myths are largely made of 'truth,' and indeed present aspects of truth that can only be received in this mode." Myths are stories that a culture believes to be true (and may be true), while the outside world believes a culture's myths to be untrue or distorted.

A New Contract: Creative Nonfiction as Personal Myth

Since CNF cannot achieve truth on the page, maybe it's time to clarify the contract between writer and reader. My call is to consider CNF to be the sharing our own personal myths rather than a sharing of our truths. If we view CNF as personal myth, we've done two things:

1. We still demand that the writer works toward truth because myths are events that the teller (or writer) believes to be abso-

lutely true. Therefore, the writer must probe memory while also reviewing outside sources to strengthen the phenomenal truths of their stories. That means that as I write my narratives of Joanne breaking up with me, I need to excavate as deeply as I can into memory (and other factual resources—old journals, photo albums, even, maybe an interview with Joanne) to tell an event as truly as possible.

2. We shift the reader's expectations from expecting truth to expecting myths that the writer believes (sincerely and completely) to be true. This shift allows the reader to understand that although the writer hopes to convey a noumenal truth, this is impossible because of (at the very least) the imaginative nature of remembering, the forgetting curve, the faultiness of eyewitness accounts, and only having access to phenomenal truths.

If writers enter the writing process knowing they need to tell the truth, while the reader knows that they are reading a myth, then we have a clear and effective contract between the two parties.

Rather than seeing CNF as a broken genre because memory is not perfect and because the noumenal truth is inaccessible, we should see CNF as a beautiful addition to the other genres because what we are reading—what we are holding in our very hands—is the writer's world as interpreted through the senses and re-envisioned through the imaginative nature of memory, which is maybe even more beautiful than any noumenal truth. And though these stories can never be perfectly true (or even approaching truth), our essays and memoirs can be something even more powerful; they can be our personal mythologies shared with our world.

The Breakup between Sean and Joanne: Her Memory

It is now many years after Joanne and I broke up and she and I are hanging out for the first time in three or four years. We decide to reconnect by spending six days canoeing the Delaware River. During the slow hours, we talk about the future and the present but also about the past. Somewhere south of the Delaware Water Gap, during the long flat stretches of river, I bring up her breaking up with me when we were teenagers.

Joanne sets the canoe paddle across her legs and looks at me as if I am crazy. She says quietly, "That's not how we first broke up." She glances at the hills that tumble into the river. "You broke up with me when we were both in high school. You said that you weren't ready for all the commitment."

"Really?" I ask. "Really?"

"Yeah, spring of your senior year, you broke up with me over the phone. I went downstairs to my sister's room and cried and cried. I was so sad, I dry heaved." Joanne pauses, looks at me, and without any meanness says, "You broke up with me first. And then I broke up with you later, once you went to East Stroudsburg. After you broke up with me, nothing was the same. I could never trust your love after that."

"Sorry," I say, meaning I am sorry for breaking up with her. I'm also sorry about having the memory all wrong, even sorrier to lose my version of that breakup—it was a part of me for so many years.

As we float down the river, neither of us paddling, I come to realize slowly and uncomfortably that now I have a new way to tell my stories, a new way to write my memories—with me as the originator of the breakup.

Joanne smile, picks up her paddle, and says, "That's okay. It was a long time ago."

We paddle onward, toward tonight's camp spot. And I think that like this canoe trip, maybe what matters the most is the exploring, the attempts at understanding. Even if we never reach our exact destination.

JUDITH KITCHEN

GONE A-SAILING: A VOYAGE TO THE EDGE OF NONFICTION (IN WHICH I FOLLOW MY OWN EXERCISE FOR WRITING ABOUT A PHOTOGRAPH)

Begin with a photograph—one that has some personal meaning: maybe a photo of your mother before she was married; an odd snapshot from the box on the shelf, someone vaguely familiar, but who?

June 14, 1930: My mother is setting sail for a month in Europe. She is twenty-three, just finished with her first years of teaching, widening her world with this whirlwind tour of too many countries in too short a time. What can we make of this girl—for surely she's still girlish as we meet her in the box of photos and the pages of the leather journal she left behind. She is not yet my mother. No, she's the young woman in the practical shoes, the one whose dark hair is hidden under her hat, the one who is singing slightly off-key.

I do not know this woman, though the handwriting is more than familiar. It follows me with its air of reproach. Who are you, to pry open the past? To judge it with your twenty-first-century knowledge? What do you know of what she didn't know? And why?

And you—who are you? Well, you have inherited the journal, and the box, and somehow you think they are yours for the milking. What is it that writers of nonfiction do, if not milk the past, the facts of the past? And these are the facts: solid in your hand, the heft of it locked in its flimsy leather cover, the scope of it scattered in its smattering of snapshots. So that's where you start—you, the writer whose job, as you see it, is to open her past and let it color your present. You open it carefully because the leather is cracked; it flakes in your hand, and the ink has already faded in places. You are careful with the book, but not with the words—you swallow the words, and you steal them, and judge. You handle your young mother roughly. She's far too innocent for your taste. Innocent, and cheerful, and fleshed out with cliché.

> We met a most charming man, Dr. Truman Gordon of Minneapolis, Minn. He is grand looking—especially in a tuxedo. He talked with us last night as we were up on deck watching the stars and he told us he was a minister. He told us one thing I shall never forget—"that God gave us memories so we could have roses in December."

See what I mean? I step from the second person and own my contempt. She's gullible, that's what she is. It's easy for me to go to Google, type in the words, find the source. "Roses in December": J. M. Barrie, Rectorial address, May 3, 1922, St. Andrew's University, Scotland. Her charming tuxedo-dressed Dr. Gordon was a bit of a fraud, passing those words off as his own—and she didn't sense it. How was she to know?

They say a photograph is worth a thousand words. Well, your job, then, is not description. It is contemplation. Speculation. Fantasy. You must surround this photograph with the thoughts and feelings that well up in you. You must probe its contents, and then move beyond its boundaries, thinking about what it doesn't say, what isn't in the frame—what you know you simply cannot know.

Where to start? I could begin with the farm where she grew up, but I choose not to. Not that I know very much about it, but somehow a farm seems, well, available. So I begin with the ship. After all, I can start anywhere, as long as I stick to the facts. But do I need to stick to the facts? They are so few. And far between. Surely distance makes room for some slippage.

There she is in the photo. Oh dear, here we go—I write the ubiquitous "I have a photo taken before my mother embarked. In it she's wearing . . ." —those thousand words the photo itself, in its black-and-white certainty, would wipe off the page. All those descriptions of photos we care almost nothing about. Let's leave them hanging on the wall where they belong.

But, I remind myself, the photo is an anchor to reality. Proof of what was. Oh really? Depends on how you want to read its tone. You want melancholy? Okay, *there she is, a little tentative in her new coat and hat, a little bit lonely in all that hustle and bustle. Clearly a farm girl out of her element. Already she misses her dog, Jack.* You want cheerful? *There she is, all dolled up with somewhere to go. She peeks out from under her stylish new cloche, dreaming of decks streaming with moonlight. She has a steamer trunk filled with clothes for every occasion. But what do you wear for moonlight?* See what I mean?

Of course the writer colors the scene; there's nothing completely objective about it. Still, it would be hard to put tears on that smiling face, so my scope is necessarily narrowed, even if just a bit. And even more when there's something other than my own desires—something concrete—to spark speculation.

> There was a movie on board—but we couldn't see—too many spectators. We danced to a rather blarey electric victrola.

Ah, that's better. Something for me to imagine into being, music drifting out into the watery night, and my mother skimming the surface of her dreams. Let's dress her up, like a paper doll. I'll give her some silver shoes with tiny straps, and a white dress that echoes the drift of the song. Can I do that, just make up her clothes? What if I say I am making them up? I don't like those sturdy black shoes in her photo. Can't I give her something to dream on? How about if I use those old stand-bys—"maybe," "perhaps," "it might be," "it could have been"? It's true—she *might* have packed a pair of dancing shoes.

It's 1930, and the Victrola is "blarey," though it *could* be the voice itself, a bit tinny, thinned to a kind of strung-out perfection. *Maybe* she's listening to Gene Austin singing "The Girl of My Dreams." And she *is* the girl of someone's dreams, if only her own. From the journal alone, I think we have enough evidence to say that.

And we have knowledge that she didn't have, not then. In just seven years Vera Lynn will be singing a song called "Roses in December" and who knows if my mother blushed, remembering how she believed what that charming man told her, way back then? Who knows if she heard a snatch of that song and turned off the Philco with a decisive *click*, closed the book on her embarrassing past? Who knows if it was a Philco? But surely the reader doesn't want me to worry about Philco versus Zenith or Crosley. Isn't the imagined Philco enough to set the tone while still being true to myself—and to her? Ah, that's the hard part: knowing just who it is I am staying true to, when what I am doing is trying to figure her out.

Look at it as a physical object. Look at its subject. Who inhabits its spaces? Ask it questions. What is your relationship to this scene? Who is taking the photograph? Where is she now in its sepia tint?

And that's the point. I do not know this woman, and yet I know who she became. I know too much and too little simultaneously. I have the verification without the nuance. One touch on the keyboard and I have history at my fingertips. But it's history without a tangled web of emotion. I have no idea what she felt. Even her diary gives detail over depth. She leaves me coldly in the dark.

Where is she in this jumble of fact that clutters my bottom shelves? I will have to make her up. But you can't just make her up, set her in motion, and see what ensues. It's not only a matter of being fair; it's a matter of why you are here in the first place, looking at the photo, trying to decipher her inscrutable smile. You're on the prowl for the roots of your past, and this is supposed to be creative nonfiction. You can't play this out as though it were invented. Because otherwise, you'll have invented your self. A self you won't recognize when you face it in the mirror.

Okay, we'll go the duller route. In my mother's album, a snapshot of seven men on the deck of a ship. They're wearing uniforms, so they must be staff of some sort. Stewards, I think they called them. Look at the debonair way they've all folded a white handkerchief and tucked it in the left pocket. Three wear hats, but the other four have let their hair fly free, or sort of free, because two of them have slicked theirs down in the style of the times. (Brylcream was invented in 1928—so these guys were up on the latest fashions.)

See how easily we can penetrate and pry? Google puts so much information at our disposal that we forget it's emotion we're after. Already I'm sick of this, the way I guess at glossing a time I call up through cyberspace. My mother's diary does a better job of capturing the transitory mood:

> The stewards are the best looking and most interesting people we have met yet. They wear dark blue uniforms with brass buttons and white caps with blue bands and gold lettering. The lounge steward is adorable—he helps to serve tea in the afternoon and he has a charming smile. The dining room steward is nice too—and the captain is dignified, stalwart and commanding looking. We learned how to put on life-savers today.

Adorable, charming, dignified. At least she knows how she feels about them. So picture her now, standing with a dozen other young women, cameras in hand, catching row upon row of brass buttons. Catching the moment that isn't a moment—not yet. It's still lost in the loose piles of prints, tucked away for eighty-two years, outliving the ship—*The Letitia*—and all the people on board.

Now come at the photograph from many angles. You can use it as a starting point, expanding until it comes alive for the reader, as it has for you. Or you can write it into being, telling its story right up to the moment of the camera's click.

Let's start with the obvious. My mother was simply one more young woman setting out on the adventure of her lifetime. Each of these men had a life. Family, friends, job, country. Children and grandchildren, yet to be born. Each one had a name, and she will possibly never learn it. Yet here they are, alive again, posed for a dozen different memories. To a man, their smiles are impersonal, rehearsed, awkward in the way that anyone is awkward standing, staged, for the camera event. And now they stand forever in this frozen moment, framed by the limits of the lens. What words can I find to move beyond its borders, touch what I know I simply cannot know?

Just how can I touch the lives that are barred from me, locked as I am in the role of observer? Surely this is not as simple as "perhaps," or "I wonder if," or "Now it seems as though." Though you, as the writer, will need those phrases—need their cautious foray into the anonymous past.

Anonymous, yes, that's true. But don't forget your mother. She is your link; you have to keep her in mind. Otherwise, go ahead, go for broke, go all the way over the edge. Write a story about a steward on a ship sailing up the St. Lawrence in June 1930. Let him think his own thoughts about that girl (surely he would have said *girl*) in those awful shoes. Let him watch her silly antics with the camera. Let him dream about Dolly, the girl he will return to, who lives in Alberta. Let him dream about Fiona, the girl he will return to when the ship docks in Glasgow. Let him tell Dolly—or Fiona—about the women who always want to line them up behind the rail like animals in a zoo, and snap. What do they do with it later?

Or let him lead her on, let *him* be the one who mentions roses in December. Let him ask her to dance. Were the stewards allowed to mix with the passengers? I'll have to look that up. Or else not. Let him begin something surreptitious, and passionate. There's nothing to stop you, is there? But wouldn't you be playing fast and loose with someone else's life? How will you feel when you've led her astray, your somewhat prim and proper mother? You might like her more, but who is it you will be liking?

Oh, how can it hurt? Give them a fling. Let her learn some of life's hard lessons. In the morning, he will look the other way. Let her learn that the man who is most attractive may be least reliable. You need to have her know this before she chooses your father. You need her to be less gullible.

See how easy it is to stray? Still, the question haunts you: how can you keep the project itself tethered to truth even as your mind ranges and ransacks its store of what-ifs and if-thens? Motive is at stake for you, no less than for a fiction writer. If you wanted a mother you did not have, why not invent her wholly, free the imagination and write a novel? But you have chosen nonfiction—a genre that may be narrower than fiction, but has its own strictures, which give it its value. It is built on the scaffold of fact, which it may not abandon. Even the essay, with its greater leeway for voice, sensibility, exploration, and play owes its fidelity to the facts it is making something of. Otherwise it loses credibility precisely where fiction gains it—in the specificity of what never happened.

There's a difference of purpose, and your purpose, as you see it, is self-knowledge, not self-invention. After all, there is the absolute fact of the artifact: seven men lined up along the deck, locked in their stance for all time. How can you honor the authenticity of this moment, this place, this genuine vessel of attention, if you deliberately look another way? There must have been a reason you were rummaging in that box, looking for a person you know you never truly knew.

You can comment on the photo, making it a central part of your written text. Move into the "tone" of the moment. Think about what the photo holds for all time. Think about the nature of time.

Prepositions. They are the secret. Look at the photo again, thinking *from*.

From this moment on, she has lost her innocence. Look at him not looking in

*her direction. He isn't even smiling. He's become simply one more man who wants
a tip. She's nothing special. She should have known. It's possible, though, that she
needed his indifference in order to meet someone else, someone who does not give
off the odor of contempt. Perhaps she will turn around and bump into a man who
does not own a tuxedo and has no fancy quotes to bandy. Someone for whom she
really is the girl of his dreams.*

Or think *to.*

*Hey you, yes you, at the far end of the frame. You with your eyes on some-
thing else, something off to the side. Look at her. See who she is. She grew up
lonely on a farm. She worked her way through high school, then college, and now
is her chance. She's worth a second glance. See those shoes—they spell someone
like you. Someone unused to the polished lemon scent of the cabin, the chime of
money on the tray. Be careful of her. She falls for the minister's stolen words. The
captain's "dignity." Be careful of her, man of too many ports, and too much savoir
faire.*

Think *around.* In *and* out.

*This is the first camera she has ever owned. She will paste this moment into a
book, tucking the corners into the holders, labeling it as though she were saving
time for someone else. And maybe she is. Maybe she plans to hand them to me,
sometime when she senses I will need what they have to say. But I come from
another world—how can she tell me of shipboard time, the way it seems to stretch
lazily out to where the ocean repeats itself. The way the days become each other,
and even a wink can seem larger than life. The way the music holds the stars in
place, and the future folds its handkerchief and tucks itself away. The way my
future seems, to her, less real than a day when shadows disappeared under the
bullion sun.*

Think *beyond.*

*You know what none of them knew on that bright day in June. You listen to
the faint sound of bootsteps that they cannot hear. Some of them—the younger
ones—will have to meet the challenge. Cut out the goofy one with the glasses;
they'll give him a job at a desk. The one next to him—with the silly mustache and
the pocket full of pens—he'll be one of the first to go. That's because he lives in
Toronto. Let him land in Britain in 1940 with the 1st Canadian Infantry Division.
For most of his service, he'll simply be on patrol—until the final D-Day landing at
Juno, where he will lose a leg. By then your mother will have married your pacifist
father, who also has a silly mustache, and his red hair is just as wild.*

There's an important distinction between invention and inventive. You haven't bent the truth so much as told it slant. Gone outside the frame. You may have toyed with detail to create a context, fabricated scene in the name of explanation, but that, you would contend, is the definition of inventive—resourcefully making use of what's at hand. The real invention is the speaking voice, the one that runs in your head and carries its own tune. The one who speaks for us in the way that Lee Martin suggests when he says, "We create ourselves as characters in our essays, people who are conflicted and trying to reach some sort of balance. We have to be able to see ourselves as clearly and with as much insight as we do the characters we create of others."

Give what you've written a context, a stance from which you are looking. Wonder about your young mother: what were her dreams? Where did they go? Give that stranger a life he may never have lived, but one that connects him to you in the odd, imaginative space that exists between you—now that you own a piece of his life.

Be honest. You've had your own flirtation. Hasn't going astray led you to something larger? Haven't you listened to other parts of yourself? Found yourself outside the box of your intentions? None of this takes you where you thought you were going as you, too, walked up the gangplank that bright day in June. But did you really know where you were going? You only know *that* when you get there. Maybe now you understand just a bit more about your mother than if you had stuck to the straight and narrow. Maybe you judge her just a bit less.

You still don't know what you didn't know, and neither nonfiction nor fiction will tell you. But somehow you sense that meaning hides in that limbo where genres blend. In that space where you are forced to give up some fact in favor of supposition, and where you pull back from fabrication in favor of something that casts a real shadow, and has a real scent.

You go back to first person, touch base with who you are—or who you want to be. Maybe that's the real question. The impetus for exploration. Who *do* you want to be? As daughter, as writer, as fellow human being? In fiction, the writer can make metaphor; in the essay, though, the writer needs to find the metaphor. Uncover it, and test its limits. So I contemplate what it could have meant to hold up the camera to seven other lives and claim them. It seems to me now that she was saving them for me.

Oliver, George, Roger, Harry, Stephen, Alan, Frank.

Or

Simon, Tony, Joseph, Norman, Terence, Rupert, David.

Or

William, Robert, Willis, James, Gerard, Stanley, Karl.

What does it matter, now that they are lost to time? But somewhere someone opens an album and finds him there—Joe—the one who went to war. Joe, who came home feeling lucky and went to work every day, wearing his new wooden leg. Someone says, "I never knew he had a mustache! Look at all that hair!" Someone for whom the game I play would be transgression. Someone for whom he (not the fictional Joe, but the man whose face summons genuine remembrance) is real as can be.

By directing your attention to the object itself, you have emerged as a narrating sensibility. By speculating, crossing that intricate divide between fiction and nonfiction, you have found those thousand words that might be worth a photograph.

There's something different to be learned on each side of the divide. By deciding that nonfiction would best serve my purpose, I knew that, no matter how much I batted my eyes at fiction, I would end up facing an external reality and that the facts—however bereft of detail or knowledge—would be at once more liberating, more mysterious. I set sail with all my mother's ingenuous expressions. I returned as myself, with her lifetime behind me. Along the way, I learned that the present shines with its own intensities, and none of us ever really knows what is about to happen. Now I am left to wonder what it is that I am innocent of. What boots or drones or fiery planes I cannot yet hear.

The young woman lifts her camera high. As though the lens could save her, she nearly cuts off the man she is aiming it at, the one who looks away as another man—the one with the impish grin—straddles his shoulder. She knows she is living a fantasy, that she will go back to the flat Midwest, back to teaching school. But for this brief instant, why shouldn't she hold him on the silver halide of her dream?

An old woman stands behind her and feels responsible to something fleeting, something so delicate it almost has no words. She has given up wanting to pronounce. Or conclude. Of course, she'd like to find a modicum of insight. But it is ephemeral. It flirts with her, then looks away. What she senses, now that she has played with fiction and pulled back, is the weight of the self that others will never comprehend. She knows what it is to have been in a place, and a time. To have thought her own thoughts, and held them accountable. She is suddenly, overwhelmingly aware that her own image, so distinct in her mind, will also become ephemeral—something to linger over in an album.

She stands behind her young not-yet-mother and watches wave upon wave upon wave, bringing the children of immigrants back to the castles and courtyards of the lands their parents came from. She knows that they will look through strangers' eyes, and then return home, as though they do not recognize what brought them to this moment. The old woman is still not sure what brought her here, to the end of a diary where, she's absolutely convinced, her mother is still wearing those horrible shoes. So why not let that girl have the last words—the ones in the confident handwriting with which the fragile book closes.

> If Thou thyself wouldst fully know,
> Then go asailing o'er the sea,
> 'Twill stir thy nature to its depths
> And bring out all there is in thee.

H. LEE BARNES

MEMORY, LANGUAGE, AND TRUTH IN THE WRITTEN MOMENT

Recently I sat as a juror in a criminal case and listened to the testimony of five witnesses to the same events. All swore to tell the truth, and all of them most likely did. Yet they witnessed the event from different perspectives and so recalled different details. The female victim of the robbery claimed to have been punched by the suspect. Another witness, who was pumping gas nearby, claimed not to have seen the punch but heard the fray, and when he looked saw the victim fighting and holding her own against the defendant. Testifying, he said that he assumed the disturbance was some kind of domestic quarrel and the defendant was the one being assaulted. Other witnesses recalled different things. All we jurors could draw from the contradictions in testimony was that human beings experience the world in complex ways and perception, which leads to memory, is a complicated filter for those experiences. Among the definitions of memory *Webster's* offers is one referencing plastics and metals: "the capacity for showing effects as to the result of past treatment or for returning to a former condition." This can be applied to human memory as well. Witnesses or participants, as in the criminal case previously described, may recall details of an event and mold them into memory as they speak the words on the witness stand. As writers of creative nonfiction, we use language to re-create (or remold) a memory into words on the page.

Ultimately, what was really on trial in that robbery case, along with the defendant, was the truth. And that was the burden placed on the jury. To find the truth. In certain ways, creative nonfiction writers are like jurors, putting memories on trial, sifting for motive and meaning, using language to re-create and re-witness, and, hopefully, discovering the truth.

Let me tell you a story, a story about the 1977 Super Bowl, the one where Kenny Stabler tossed completion after completion to Fred Belitnikoff and Clarence Davis rushed for gain after gain, while on the opposing side Fran Tarkenton was harried by a swarm of determined Oakland defenders. A pretty, ponytailed redhead named Patty was my date at that Super Bowl, and there was a plainclothes security man there who kept telling me to stop taking silk flowers from the trellis that served as a passage to the VIP tables. I remember the party clearly, even what we both wore that night: she, a white dress with three rows of ruffles on the skirt—fashionable at the time—and I, a burnt-autumn wool suit with wide lapels. Can I recall every detail of that night? No. The words exchanged? No. But I can reconstruct it in some clear fashion because it was the only Super Bowl I ever attended, and because that pretty redhead thanked me for the bouquet of silk flowers I pilfered off the trellis and then dismissed me that night from her porch without so much as a kiss.

It seems reasonable to assume that as humans evolved, our brains became hardwired to store information as a function of survival. And as human society evolved we learned to use our memories as a means to steer our way through the social labyrinth. A pretty redhead closing a door sends a clear message to the one left on the steps that she's not interested—information stored for future dating. (At least it wasn't a handshake.) Like memory, language is hardwired in us as a tool of survival as well. Science tells us language and memory are both deep structures embedded in our DNA. Intuition tells us they are inherently interlinked as social tools and both have power over us in determining what we say or don't say in a given situation, how we interpret and internalize the moment, and how we relive that very experience. If Patty had said something memorable at the door, such as thanking me for a wonderful time and "Please call," I might have followed up. As it was, she offered a simple thank-you and goodnight, and I stood under a glaring porch light wondering what I'd done wrong. That moment crystallized the evening, an otherwise wonderful night that ended not with an exclamation point but an ellipsis followed by a question mark, a sort of training tape for future reference that plays out in words that were or weren't spoken.

If memories are stored in files somewhere in our gray matter, language is the medium we use to sort through those files. Let's take the case of the man who twice sees a tiger in the area where he gathers reeds to make baskets. This information is vital to how he'll behave in future journeys to the marsh. It's also information he can pass on to others, who in turn will pass it on to still others. This overly simplified example describes the relationship of event and memory and language as co-functions in preserving, retrieving, and transmitting information. Language is also the tool we use to puzzle out both current problems and the annoying past that insists on tripping clumsily into our present thoughts.

In translating an experience onto a page, writers sometimes rely on comparison in the form of simile, metaphor, or other figurative use of language to create an impression or capture an image. But figurative language doesn't always serve a particular memory well. Diesel fuel is often cited as being among the stimuli that most arouses a PTSD reaction in Vietnam veterans. Some have severe episodes when exposed to it. But diesel fuel smells the way it does; it refuses comparison. How does one re-create pain in words? Or capture degrees of pain or pleasure?

The best we can do in re-creating the sensual is to form a mongrel version of it, which is also what we do with an experience. Writers must sometimes rely on a reader's ability to make connections. Whether drawing the material from the imagination, life experience, or witnesses, the writer digs beneath the surface of the experience and translates the external event or memory into something fuller, which is to say, the material is presented in such a way that it is felt and understood by a reader as honest human interaction and reaction taking place in a fully realized, sensual world. A writer's goal is assembling the material into language *felt* to be true so that the reader will then experience the written moment in some personal and meaningful way.

In writing *Dummy Up and Deal*, a book that captures a broad range of stories from casino dealers in Las Vegas, I listened to dealers tell stories at parties and in the dealers' break rooms and I jotted them down. As I began assembling the stories, I saw that using a straight journalistic approach would not capture either individual personalities or the culture of the business. To be felt, the work had to be true to the dealers' memories, and yet stretch beyond the boundaries of journalism. Some stories seemed to translate best to first person and some third. When writing more elaborate stories, I also had to create a voice for them and in several cases find the *real* story and give those stories a narrative shape.

One case in particular was that of a baccarat dealer who wanted only to tell about a tip of several thousand dollars he and his crew had scored off a high roller he called The Sweetheart. At first, the story seemed just another anecdote, big money gambled freely, resulting in a huge tip. Over a few cups of coffee the dealer, who came from a humble background in a small town in Arkansas, sprinkled the conversation with a scattering of memories, experiences that he couldn't fathom as a coherent whole. After dropping out of high school while in his teens and starting a family, he barely eked by on his wages as a construction laborer. Seeking a better lot, he moved his family to Las Vegas. Their first week in town they stayed in a motel near the Strip, where they woke one morning to the news that a toddler was found drowned in the swimming pool. The man eventually drifted into casino work, learning first to deal craps, then much later dealing high-limit baccarat games. The money coming from his tips in the baccarat pit exceeded anything he'd ever imagined earning.

In the conversation his focus was on the amount of that one big tip. What he didn't see as important was what followed: the impact of that money on his family. Despite his wife and children's urgings, he refused to build a swimming pool in his backyard for fear of having a child drown in it. Instead of indulging their wants or buying an expensive car, as other dealers had, he opened tuition accounts for his children, both of whom later graduated from college. The Sweetheart continued to gamble at Caesars, and the baccarat dealer enjoyed several more scores. When word came that The Sweetheart had died from a sudden heart attack, the dealer flew to Los Angeles for the funeral, the only one on his crew to do so.

The dealer thought of his varied experiences as conversational bits to be passed along over a cup of coffee. He failed to see how the memories—the drowned child, his fears for his own children, another man's generosity, the wise use of the unexpected money—coalesced as elements of a story. The shaping I did of those disparate bits of disconnected memories resulted in a small piece that touched on larger human themes. To give it a sense of verisimilitude the story begged to be told in a first-person voice and to use language that captured his colloquial speech. It had to read as if it came directly from a man giving testimony to his experience. When the dealer read the finished story, he clasped my arm and thanked me, saying that was how the story was "in my head, but not in my mouth."

In similar ways, we creative nonfiction writers shape stories from our own lives, especially from memories that shadow us. Writing a memoir isn't just about recalling and rendering memories, but about seeing our memories as a coherent whole, about searching for some truth that's larger than us. Through language we re-create past events somewhat like the remolding of metal or plastic that the *Webster's* definition above refers to. What *Webster's* doesn't say is that metal or plastic reshaped can't duplicate precisely the original form. Our effort is aimed not just at dependably re-creating experience, but in using language that makes it engaging. Creative nonfiction conjures magic much like the illusion of a human elevated or sliced in half on a stage by a magician. No experience can be reproduced precisely, but the best memoirs reproduce it in images and thoughts rendered with language that sustains *an illusion.*

Two decades later, and a few years after we had both moved back to Las Vegas, I ran into that redhead again. In the interim, she'd married, earned a degree in accounting, became a mother, divorced, and taken to cutting her hair short. She said that she had fond memories of the Super Bowl party we attended and that she'd kept the bouquet for many years after, though she wasn't sure what ultimately had happened to it. She didn't recall opening the door to her apartment and turning around for a quick thank-you before stepping inside and closing it. She couldn't recall the end of the evening at all.

As I consider that Super Bowl and its aftermath, I'm looking for something in the muddle of memories to mold into a meaningful story. Was Patty's version less truthful than mine? Was mine tainted by expectations she didn't share? Did I hesitate because she gave me no sign? Did she give me a sign, and I missed it? Was what happened or didn't happen on that porch determined by some earlier action or inaction on my part? How did her white dress, the bouquet of colorful silk flowers held close to her breast, and her red hair aglow in the bare porch light affect my feelings? Should I have reached for her hand and told her how lovely she was? Now I'm searching these mixed memories, wondering if I can mold the event into that cohesive and coherent thing called the written moment, that thing we construct in language that transports readers out of their world and into the world of story.

KIM BARNES

THE ART AND ABSENCE OF REFLECTION IN PERSONAL NONFICTION: WHAT IS THE WHY?

> The story is my truest possession and I burnish and hammer it and wrestle it to make it whole. In return it offers me back to myself, it holds what I cannot, its embrace and memory larger than mine, more permanent . . . I didn't understand that fusing my life to the narrative, giving myself to the story's life, would be what would allow me to live.
>
> —Mark Doty

Who am I, and why? This is the question that writers of personal nonfiction must ask of themselves. Like other forms of art, the writing of memoirs and personal essays should be a journey of discovery. If we believe that we know the answer to the question before we sit down to write, we will learn nothing new about ourselves and, worse, our readers will be denied the opportunity to learn something new about themselves. Readers of your nonfiction should come away knowing more about themselves than they do about *you*.

This is true of any successful artistic endeavor—music, sculpture, dance. It's easy enough to observe that the best of literary fiction, for instance, accomplishes just this thing through the presentation of form and content and the engagement of two paralleling arcs: the arc that is action, and the arc that is emotion.

Writers of creative nonfiction, however, face a further task: How to write a narrative of discovery and surprise when (for the most part) we already know what happened. We think we may have a grip on the action of our story through memory, photos, journals, research, and interviews. But it's the emotional arc rather than the action arc of our life stories that defines their literary aspirations and success. It's not *what* happened, but *why*. It's not *what* you remember, but *why* you remember what you do. It's not *what* you're telling us, by *why* you are telling us. This is why you don't need to create fictional material to fill your narrative arc. Just as is the case with literary fiction, the imaginative leap in nonfiction is at the level of craft, not at the level of plot. You must have faith in the process of discovering the *why* of your story.

When writing your personal narratives, you must always be aware of your reader's first question: Why is she telling me this? It's the question that you must ask yourself: Why am I telling them this? Sometimes, the answer to that question lies in the textual contemplation of what you've already produced on the page—reflection in some form, which provides pacing, texture, complexity, depth, and vertical versus horizontal movement in your narrative. Tone, metaphor, point of view, tense, chronological structure, syntax, diction, foreshadowing, backstory, white space—all are tools in your toolbox. Reflection is another tool. If you apprentice yourself to the art and learn well, these tools will always be at your disposal so that if called upon to produce an adze, you can do so, and you will know how to use it appropriately. If you're constructing a steel building, you won't need an adze. The tools must fit the construction.

And you must remember this: even though what you're writing is your personal story, it is not about *you*. It's about the human condition, and it's about the art that will allow you to observe and depict that condition. It's not about the house you lived in as a child but about the house you are building on the page. As a writer of personal nonfiction, your service must first and foremost be *not* to your experience and emotions but to the *art* that your story is in the service of. Your memories, experiences, family histories—all make up the physical world of your story, and the presentation of the *what* in a specific, sophisticated, and intentional manner is essential stuff.

But what of the *why?*

Back to that adze, a word I love to say. It puts me in the mind of poetry. Award-winning author Julia Alvarez once noted that the personal essay is much closer to poetry than it is to prose. When talking about personal essays and literary memoirs (as opposed to the linear autobiographies of the famous and infamous—*I was born and I'm not yet dead*), we might briefly consider three of the ways in which poems present themselves: as narratives, as lyrics, and as meditations. Just so, the writing of personal nonfiction can take on different structures, tones, and styles. As is the case with any piece of good writing, a work of creative nonfiction must be aware of itself and understand how all of its parts are working toward a singular effect.

A narrative essay necessarily is going to be made up of a great deal of the *what*, and by this I mean re-created action. Author and sage William Kittredge often says that such essays are made up of 97 percent scene, either retold or enacted. As a narrative, it must abide by the general rules of narrative construction and be built with the appropriate tools: we need to be set in time and place; we need to know who our characters are and get them up on the stage; we must have physical movement and momentum; we must have rising action and conflict and resolution. It is in narrative essays and memoirs that we most often see the hammer marks of reflection pounded in between the scenes—that remaining 3 percent, the contemplative glue that holds the scenes together.

The lyric essay, on the other hand, exists not in the service of action but in the service of resonating image and music. How is it different from poetry, then? Maybe only in this: the poet Dick Hugo once noted that if poetry is a battle between music and meaning, let music win. I'd suggest that, with lyrical prose, meaning must win the day.

Both lyric and meditative essays often follow the path of what writer Cynthia Ozick calls "the mazy mind": the Romantic impulse to recollect and observe emotion in tranquility, to ponder and muse. It is through the Romantics, in fact, that we can get a larger sense of the role of reflection in personal writing because it was with the rise of romanticism that we saw a rebirth and redirection of the confessional. If you consider the roots of personal nonfiction, you'll observe that it was composed in the spirit of true confession, meaning in the context of spiritual self-exploration and purgation. Remember, too, that in its strict literary definition, "confessional" is not an observation of secret sins but an exploration of the life of the emotions.

The secular confessional, however, is a relatively new and mostly American form. Its focus on "the cult of the individual" often brings it bad reviews. It is sometimes coarse and vulgar but, if written with attention to craft rather than content, it can be sharp, sophisticated, and invigorating. In its most contemporary presentation—a presentation being explored and defined by younger and younger authors—we find less and less reflection, and why should we be surprised? Traditionally, memoir—from the Latin for memory—was written by people old enough to look *back* on their lives, to reminisce, to have the necessary distance to project upon their own experiences a narrative of meaning—in other words, context and self awareness.

Where, then, does this leave the twenty- and thirty-somethings who have less chronological and emotional distance from their short personal histories? How can we insist that they create intellectual context for events and emotions that will take them years to make sense of? The author and editor John D'Agata declares the essays written by such relatively young authors as Lia Purpura, Ander Monson, and David Foster Wallace to be the first new American art form since jazz. Like jazz, such essays rely on missing notes and resonating riffs. They interpret and explore the white space in, around, and outside the main melody. Part of their brilliance is that they maintain our sense and awareness of that melody even in its absence. (And I'm thinking of another quote from Hugo: "All truth must conform to music.")

Bottom line: no matter the form, style, and tone, a work of creative nonfiction must introduce and resolve emotional, intellectual, and structural tension. The use of reflection in creative nonfiction, just as in fiction, can heighten or deplete this tension, which is why writers must use it judiciously and be aware of all the different ways in which reflection can manifest itself. Because here is the thing to remember: the absence of reflection can in and of itself *be* reflection. In the absence of reflection, you must rely on other elements of craft to provide context, just as an open-domed cathedral must rely on something other than trusses and crossbeams to hold up its construction. It's not that the supporting framework isn't there: it's just in a different form.

How many ways are there to design a house? As many ways as can be imagined. Just so with the essay. Reflection is the way in which you shine the light of *why* onto the *what* of the essay. But how to let that light in? A series of squares cut in a linear pattern that punch through the dark at regular intervals? Stained glass windows that color the light and create a palette of suggested illumination? Or how about one of those tubular skylights that, via a series of canted mirrors, reflects the reflection of the reflection of the sun? Just as is the case with any element of craft, reflection cannot exist in a void. What I mean is that reflection must work in harmony with other elements of craft to produce a work of unity and integrity. It's not that clerestory windows can't be in unity with the construction of a Sears and Roebuck bungalow. It's that they can't exist outside of the harmony and integrity of the house as a whole. They need to be echoed in some other element of the house's design or decor. Consider the recent study whose goal was to discover the universal appeal of Mozart. The answer? Symmetry. We crave symmetry. Listen to the great musicians talk about the hidden symmetry of jazz.

This simply means that if an essay or memoir begins conventionally, we will expect it to proceed conventionally. We will expect physical context, our W's—who, what, when, where—answered, and what risks the texts takes to be in keeping with its construct. Again, we're simply talking about the kind of harmony of form and content that made Aristotle wet his toga. Any text, whether music or story, must teach us how to *read* it.

Consider poet Nick Flynn's critically acclaimed memoir, *Another Bullshit Night in Suck City,* which begins: "*Please,* she whispers, *how may I help you? The screen lights up with her voice. A room you enter, numbers you finger, heated, sterile almost. The phone beside her never rings, like a toy, like a prop. My father lifts the receiver in the night, speaks into it, asks, Where's the money? asks, Why can't I sleep? asks, Who left me outside?*"

From the first sentence—the voice that denies context, the second-person point of view—you understand that you are in a building whose design you many never have seen before. You understand that you must leave your preconceived notions of memoir at the door. You are taught by the text to quit expecting what you expect. Nonetheless, you recognize that you are in a building, a construct, and you either trust the author to keep the roof from falling in on your head or you don't. It's the self-awareness of Flynn's writing, a sense of its sure intent, his control of the tools, that teaches you to trust: *I'm going to mess with you here, but it's going to pay off. Just stay with me. I will guide you.*

Because we're immediately disabused of our expectation of convention, we understand that we are not going to be in a linear story and that the traditional use of reflection and reminiscence may not be present. What, then, will come in to give the story context and meaning?

Along with tone, point of view, diction, and dramatic presentation, Flynn uses one-page chapters, the script of a play, a rambling list of drinking euphemisms strung together without capitalization or punctuation, and nearly every other conceivable form to create his narrative, which serves as implied intellectual reflection: *because my history is one of chaos, betrayal, denial, aban-donment, and subterfuge, I don't know how to build and enter the house of my own story. I'm going to attempt various doors and windows and maybe the cellar. Just stay close and follow me.*

Sometimes, a simple tapping of the keyboard can open up literal and figurative space on the page. Remember that, as Derrida and others have pointed out, white space is an integral and telling part of the text. Often, it is in the white space that meaning resides. Consider Lia Purpura's lyric essay "Autopsy Report": "I shall begin with the chests of drowned men, bound with ropes and diesel-slicked. Their ears sludge-filled. Their legs mud-smeared. Asleep below deck when a freighter hit and the river rose inside their tug. Their lashes white with river silt."

What are you being taught to expect? The archaic phrasing "I shall" leads immediately into a brutal image, and the two together create tension and a sense of heightened emotion. And then white space—not just a paragraph break, but a vacant space nearly as large as the paragraph itself. In other words, the meaning of the white space weighs as much as the meaning of the text.

And then another snippet of narrative. And then white space. It might be a narrative poem, or a poetic narrative, but it tells a factual personal story. As the story progresses, the white space thins and the narrative takes up more and more of our visual space as it gains prosaic momentum and meaning so that by page 4 our white space is almost wholly gone. We have cut our way through the shallow skin of the essay. We are deep into its body, working our way through its dense musculature to the heart. What reflection we have is not the reflection of an older woman looking back on her youth but of a youthful narrator peering at herself in the *now*, the present of the experience, which defines the emotional immediacy of the narrative. When Purpura admits to laughing at the body's opening, she writes, "And now that I've admitted laughing, I shall admit this, more unexpected, still: When the assistant opened the first body up, what stepped forth, unbidden, was calm. . . . The opening was familiar. As if I'd known before, this . . . what? language? Like a dialect spoken only in childhood . . ."

"Autopsy Report" becomes a kind of *ars poetica*, a conventional form whose context is of a higher inquiry than self: it is an inquiry into the very nature of the creation of narratival meaning. Purpura brings her intellect to bear upon the experience and in doing so creates context, but it's important to note the elements of craft that we might not have expected: the use of white space, as noted, but also the use of present tense and diction to set the tone, which is a tone of self-contemplation and meditation. Again, as the essay progresses into a sense of its purpose, as it finds its way, Purpura finds herself able to articulate and reflect: "I'd seen how easily we open, our skin not at all the boundary we're convinced of as we bump into each other and excuse ourselves." It's about connection, then, to the dead and to the living, to the base aspects of our existence.

But what of Paul Auster's short piece "Why Write?" A segmented essay in five parts, it offers a series of straightforward, narrative vignettes, memories very simply told, whose context might elude us if not for the title and the final few sentences: "If nothing else, the years have taught me this: if there's a pencil in your pocket, there's a good chance that one day you'll feel tempted to start using it." The ending he gives us is nearly farcical, and if you haven't observed Auster's mind at work, you might judge it to be naive. But, of course, the essay is about much more than this: it's about the random nature of our existence, about how moments add up to meaning, about how we create functional narratives to make sense of the chaos of our lives. But Auster never mentions these things—he doesn't reflect on their meaning. It is in what he *doesn't* say that we see how the parts of his equation add up to the title's answer. It is the precise and mathematical construction of the essay that serves as commentary on the content, and it does so through the use of irony and yet another level of meaning, one that requires that *we* as readers bring our intellect to bear: as a postmodern writer, Auster is fascinated not just with story but with commentary on story. He has a particular fascination with conventional forms. If you pay attention to your archetypal sensors, you will intuit and observe that Auster's essay follows the most basic of dramatic formats: the five-act play. Exposition, rising action, climax or turning point, falling action, and denouement. By segmenting itself into five sections, it is teaching you how to read it. The tension between staid archetypal form and seemingly disconnected content is intellectual reflection that resides in the white space.

To further illustrate the ways in which reflection may present or absent itself, I want to offer romance in three forms. First, Susan Minot's short story "Lust," in which we have a first-person narrator reciting her sexual résumé as a series of seemingly random memories told in present tense, sometimes pulling you in with a swing into second person: "Leo was from a long time ago, the first one I ever saw nude . . . Roger was fast . . . You'd try to wipe off the table . . . and Willie would untuck your shirt and get his hands up under in front . . ." It's a commentary on the sexuality of women, although it never tells us this: the story doesn't reflect on itself. The speaker simply tells us the story in a tone and manner that suggests that what she's withholding may be more important than what she's confiding. But there are moments in which self-awareness begins to break through, and our relationship to the story begins to change. Without this movement, we have no story. What begins as a kind of randy romp through her grocery list of sexual trysts takes a turn toward desperation: "You wait till they come to you. . . . Then they get mad after, when you say enough is enough. . . . After sex, you curl up like a shrimp, something deep inside of you ruined . . ." It is the changing tone of the story rather than an injection of deep contemplation that indicates the speaker's dawning self-awareness.

So, too, in nonfiction. Brenda Miller, in her essay "The Date," uses the *absence* of reflection to suggest her narrative's larger meaning: "A man I like is coming for dinner. This means I sleep very little, and I wake up in the half-light of dawn, disoriented, wondering where I am. I look at my naked body stretched diagonally across the bed; I look at the untouched breasts, the white belly, and I wonder. I don't know if this man will ever touch me, but I wonder." Again, we see the use of present tense, which teaches us we won't be able to rely on reflection to give us meaning. Reflection requires distance. Present tense disallows distance. It is in this desire to stay in the moment that we find tension and meaning.

As Miller continues her preparations for the arrival of her date, we understand that she is having the kind of argument that Yeats declared to be the most important—the argument with yourself. She wants intimacy and companionship; she doesn't want to lose her solitude and independence. After all of her preparation and self-analyzing, after she fixes her hair in five different ways and dabs perfume behind her knees, after wondering whether or not she should make up her bed with fresh sheets and imagining the intimacy she craves, her date never arrives. Whether or not the date will appear and what romance might ensue is the *false* tension of the essay. The true tension is in the process of self-exploration that is not simply about Brenda but about us as well. What lengths will we go to in order to not be alone? If we allow ourselves to be subsumed by longing, in what form do we continue to exist? What part of ourselves are we willing to let go of to stay in our familiar house, keep to our known routine? Perhaps it's better to take off our new dress, step out of our fancy underpants, crawl back in between the limp and musky sheets alone, smelling only of our known selves. An author's decision to bypass expository reflection and to rely instead on other elements of craft to generate an atmosphere of contemplation creates a "climate" of emotional irony and tension—a liminal space between action and thought wherein the story resides.

And a final note: in your quest for meaning through personal narrative, you must teach yourself how to read your *own* story. You must understand how your own personal mythologies are reflected in the mythologies of people of every place and time. In order to reflect, whether through style, structure, or rhetoric, you must have an awareness of the archetypal stories that have shaped us all—the stories in which we continue to reside. In order to write first-person narratives that resonate, your stories must, through the imagination application of craft, transcend the personal. You cannot simply be a citizen of your own life; you must be a citizen of the world.

ERIK REECE

THE ACT OF WRITING:
SPEAK AND BEAR WITNESS

I did not go to eastern Kentucky looking to get mauled by bulldozers or pummeled by rocks that rain from the sky when mountains are blown apart. In the beginning, I went to the broadleaf forests of central Appalachia—the most biologically diverse ecosystems in North American—to write poetry. More specifically, I would drive from my home in Lexington, Kentucky, to Robinson Forest, a 15,000-acre woodland in the eastern part of the state. There I would spend days and weeks living in a chestnut cabin, meandering along Kentucky's cleanest streams and up some of its steepest slopes. It was John Clare, I believe, who said he didn't write his poems, but simply found them lying in the fields. Wandering the mountains and streams of Robinson Forest, I amused myself by thinking that poems would come just as easily to me. And why not? I had retreated into just about the deepest pastoral seclusion one can find in the state of Kentucky. In another culture, in another time, these magnificent oaks might have constituted a goddess's sacred grove. Certainly some semblance of the muse had to be hovering over my shoulder.

I knew, of course, there was a terrible machine rumbling at the outskirts of this woodland garden. When I was a kid, my great-grandparents owned a clothing store in the nearest town, Hazard, and when we drove down to visit them I could see along the roadside the great gashes that bulldozers had cut into the mountains. I knew what strip mining was, and I knew it was thought to be as inevitable to eastern Kentucky as poverty and kudzu. Few people questioned it, and as I said, I hadn't gone to Robinson Forest looking to cause trouble, or to get into any. Just the opposite, in fact. I was hoping that the inscrutable spirits of the natural world might still my own restless, urban nature. Like Transcendentalists of the nineteenth century, I believed—and still believe—in the power of the great god Pan. And if a hot July afternoon found me lying flat on my back in a shallow stream, then that was all the baptism I needed.

All of that changed in 2002. While staying in Robinson Forest that summer, I spent some time with a group of wildlife biologists who were reintroducing an elk herd into eastern Kentucky. But as I would come to learn, these were not the eastern elk that had been hunted to extinction in 1867. These were Rocky Mountain elk, shipped in from Colorado, and because of that, the unnatural landscape of a strip mine looked much more native to them than the dense forest preferred by the original eastern elk. Which is to say, I ended up spending far more time wandering around strip jobs than I ever thought I would. But by then, no one really used the term "strip mining" anymore. It seemed like everyone, particularly environmentalists, had started to call the practice "mountaintop removal." And from what I was beginning to see, the new label was far more accurate, even if it sounded misleadingly clinical. This wasn't the auger mining of my childhood, when only the sides of a mountain were cut away. Now coal operators where mixing ammonium nitrate and fuel oil together to literally blast to pieces the entire summit of a mountain and dump everything that wasn't coal into the streams and rivers below.

One day after tracking a young elk herd with the wildlife biologists, I climbed to the top of the fire tower in Robinson Forest. I had done this many times before to watch the sun set and the fog move in. But for some reason, on that day it struck me that Robinson Forest was an island of life surrounded by the deadest, most barren landscapes east of the Sonoran Desert. Standing at the top of the fire tower, I suddenly understood that I could no longer write about the untrammeled beauty of Robinson Forest without also writing about the forces at work to destroy it.

That has become a kind of creation story for me. Any success I have had as an "environmental writer" (a term I don't particularly like) came because of what I experienced standing at the top of the fire tower and what I did after I climbed down. Specifically, I went to the Office of Natural Resources in Frankfort, Kentucky, and started perusing permits for mountaintop removal jobs. The bound permits were all about fifteen inches thick and written in a dense, impenetrable language. I could make little of it. All I knew—and I knew this only intuitively—was that I had to write something about the perils of mountaintop removal. But I wasn't a mining engineer, I wasn't a biologist, I wasn't a lawyer, I wasn't a regulator, I wasn't a legislator, I wasn't a hydrologist, I wasn't an activist. I wasn't even a journalist, unless you count the music reviews I wrote for my college newspaper back in the late '80s. In short, I possessed none of the expertise that seemed necessary to understanding the complexities of MTR. But then, haplessly flipping through one permit, I pulled out a map. It showed, with a perforated line, the original contour of a mountain. Then with two flat lines, it showed what the peak would look like after coal operators lopped off its top. In the space between the flat lines and the jagged, perforated lines were two words in capital letters: LOST MOUN-TAIN. At last, here was something I did know how to do—perceive irony. If the coal operators had their way, they would decapitate Lost Mountain, and it would be, well, lost. Not lost in the sense that it couldn't be found, but lost in the sense that it could never be recovered. It would be rendered irretrievable, destroyed, killed. Sitting alone among those sagging shelves of permits, I suddenly knew I would write a book called *Lost Mountain*.

Beyond my attenuated sense of irony, I thought I had two more things going for me. I was a pretty good observer of detail—I had learned that from my mentor, Guy Davenport—and I could tell a decent story. Given that I could claim no expertise on the subject of strip mining, I decided I would simply try to tell, through direct observation, the story of one mountain. I would climb it at least once a month for a year, and I would recount, firsthand, the story of its destruction. Having seen the permit map, I knew how the story would end. It would end badly. But I didn't know—and due to the steep contours of the mountains and the secrecy of the coal industry—hardly anyone else knew, what happened between the felling of the first tree and the rooting out of the last block of coal. So I went to see.

Though I worked hard to learn from journalists I admired, I didn't want to write a journalistic account exactly. Instead I tried to approach Lost Mountain the way I had first entered Robinson Forest: I wanted to see the flora and fauna with the eye of an amateur naturalist and the disposition of a Romantic poet. I wanted to create a portrait of Lost Mountain that might stir certain feelings for the place, a sense of affinity that went beyond some abstract idea that preserving abstract "nature" is a good thing to do. Even though I knew it was too late for Lost Mountain, I wanted to show, as clearly as I could, what was being destroyed and why other Appalachian mountains should be preserved.

But to create such a portrait of Lost Mountain, I obviously had to see it up close, and that meant I had to trespass. (A few years later, I heard the president of the Kentucky Coal Association tell a group of students that I had set a terrible moral example for them.) I had to sneak past the mine gates or up the backside of the mountain. I had to dodge the omnipresent white pickup trucks that signified mine foremen or supervisors. And I had to try and not get hit by detonated debris that the industry rather benignly calls "flyrock." I suppose one could call this the work of an investigative reporter, but that's not really how it felt. Instead, I understood myself to be inscribing a tombstone, as Edward Abbey said of his book *Desert Solitaire*, and I wanted it to be a grave one indeed, a weight that, in Abbey's words, could be thrown "at something big and glassy."

At the beginning, I took a lot of field notes, sketching the tracks of deer, raccoons, turkey, and foxes. I explored the rich ecological communities that lived in and around the capstones of Lost Mountain. I watched and listened to ovenbirds and wood thrushes flitting through the understory of the mountain's oak-hickory canopy. Once, by mistake, I even picked up a copperhead—thankfully, a cold and lethargic one. I often did these things on the backside of the mountain, where the headwaters of Lost Creek come alive. One spring day, I was standing in deep, damp shade, writing the words "spotted trillium" in my notebook, when an explosion shook the entire mountain and I fell, startled, into Lost Creek. And that, as much as anything, represented the sorry contradiction I wanted to capture—North America's most biologically diverse ecosystem being blown asunder by the forces that power our culture of acquisitive convenience.

I eventually got to know Lost Mountain so well that I could be standing, unnoticed, about thirty feet from a bulldozer that was busy scraping away one of its sandstone spurs. Hiding behind a large chestnut oak, the last one left before the ridgeside plunged into a cratered pit, I could make out the tattoos on the driver's arm. And usually, at the end of the day, after the dozer had shut down and the strip miners were gone, I would sit on the large capstone at the top of Lost Mountain and take it all in. The Carolina wrens and red-eyed vireos would start singing again as I sat in the quiet of late afternoon and tried to get my head around what I was seeing. F. Scott Fitzgerald once said the sign of a good mind is that it can hold two opposing thoughts at once. But I could never do that up on Lost Mountain. I couldn't let the industrial thought that was destroying this place sit beside the ecological thought that said the mountain knows what it's doing, and had been doing it for a few billion years before someone with opposable thumbs got around to inventing a D-11 dozer. I decided that more important than holding in mind two irreconcilable thoughts was seizing on one of those thoughts and turning it into words, into action. In the end, I can say that my experience on Lost Mountain turned me into a Jamesian pragmatist—someone who believes a thought isn't really *worth* having unless it can be converted into an act of conscience.

Is writing such an act? I think it can be. I wouldn't call what I wrote about Lost Mountain a strict act of advocacy or activism any more than I would call it a strict act of journalism. But seventy years ago in "The Land Ethic," which is to my thinking the most important piece of twentieth-century American nonfiction, Aldo Leopold set down the guiding principles for how we might resign our roles as conquerors of the natural world and instead become members of a land community: "A thing is right when it tends to preserve the integrity, stability and beauty of the biotic community. It is wrong when it tends otherwise." This clear and profound distinction between right and wrong, between the ethical and the unethical, can carry us quite far when it comes to thinking about acts of conscience (what is mountaintop removal if not the ultimate act of *dis*-integration, *in*-stability and ugliness). And any writing about the land and its people that proceeds from Leopold's premise will be such an act, and it will likely inspire other acts that take many other forms beyond writing.

One of the great embodiments of such a writerly act of conscience took place eighty years ago, not far from Lost Mountain. In 1931, coal industry gun thugs surrounded the house of a union organizer named Sam Reece, hoping to ambush him. They waited all night. Reece never came home, but inside the house, his wife Florence tore a page down from a wall calendar, and huddled on the floor with her children, she wrote the twentieth century's most famous union song, "Which Side Are You On?" Written to the tune of the traditional ballad "Lay the Lily Low," the song takes on the brutal Harlan County sheriff J. H. Blair, and the violent men he deputized to kill union miners. The last three verses go like this:

They say in Harlan County,
There are no neutrals there.
You'll either be a union man,
Or a thug for J. H. Blair.
Oh, workers can you stand it?
Oh, tell me how you can.
Will you be a lousy scab,
Or will you be a man?
Don't scab for the bosses,
Don't listen to their lies.
Us poor folks haven't got a chance,
Unless we organize.

Then comes the chorus, which simply repeats the question of the title over and over: "Which side are you on, boys, which side are you on?" I've sung that anthem at many rallies, often with verses updated to reflect the contemporary struggles of the coalfields. One of the song's many virtues is clarity. It says that one side has the power and one side does not. And, unfortunately, the later is the side of conscience. So the only way to take hold of the power wielded by the coal operators is to act—to act together, to act on principle, and to act in public.

Thus the composing of "Which Side Are You On?" was a solitary act that has inspired great acts of solidarity. Writing *is* a solitary act—but it's only the first act. What comes next is what really matters. However, personally, I have never been all that comfortable with the second act. I'm a solitary person by nature and not much of a joiner. Yet still I've come to see the nonfiction writer's solitary act as important to the greater cause—really the only cause—of decreasing cruelty and increasing sympathy. In that service, nonfiction writers can perform two fundamental tasks that are unavailable to the writers of fiction. Like Florence Reece, we can bear witness and we can call for change—for an end to injustices.

It is precisely on this subject of bearing witness that I find John D'Agata's recent writing about the genre of nonfiction so malicious and inept. D'Agata argues that nonfiction must serve the greater good of art, and therefore reality can be altered in the name of art. But to elevate reality to the level of art is one of the fundamental tasks of the nonfiction writer, and to say it cannot be done honestly, as D'Agata claims, displays an astonishing lack of imagination as well as an equally unflattering amount of arrogance and pedantry. But let's put aside the either-or nature of this line of thinking. The real problem here is that such an attitude robs nonfiction of it greatest strength and virtue—its ability to bear witness and the veracity that comes from that act. To admit that one only has a passing interest in representing reality is to forfeit one's moral authority to call that reality into question. That is to say, I have no right to call mountaintop removal an injustice—one in need of a new reality—if I cannot be trusted to depict the travesty of strip mining as it now exists. To play D'Agata's game is to lose the reader's trust, and without that, it seems to me that the nonfiction writer has very little left. Writers of that persuasion can align themselves with Picasso's famous sentiment that art is the lie that tells the truth, but I have no truck with such pretentiousness. The work of the nonfiction writers I most admire is telling a truth that exposes a lie.

This makes the nonfiction writer a close cousin to the documentary filmmaker. The documentarian's images are vitally important, especially to a cause like mountaintop removal where everyone needs to *see* a mountain being blasted to rubble. But the written word works on the brain in ways very different from, though complementary to, the visual image. If the visual image is more immediate, more visceral, the word provides the reader with the time and the space to linger, cogitate, and wrestle with the implications of what was just said. The reader invests in the work of prose in a way that is often more deliberate and more engaged than with film—which may explain why the brain is most active when reading than at any other time, except dreaming.

I've been called a dreamer quite a lot since writing *Lost Mountain*. Only in this context, the term usually means that I'm someone who is used to losing. And that's true. For the environmental writer, losing is simply an occupational hazard. But the appropriate response to Florence Reece's "Which Side Are You On?" is not, "I'm on the side that's going to win," but rather, "I'm on the side of conscience, empathy, and affection."

Because my last name has the same unusual spelling as Florence Reece's (with a *c* instead of an *s*), people sometimes ask if I'm related to her. Unfortunately, I've never been able to prove a family connection, but in any case, that's the side I'm on—the side of Florence and Sam Reece, the side of the mountain, the side of the men and women who are dying because the air and the water around Appalachian strip mines isn't fit to breathe and drink. If that's the losing side, then it simply means there is more work to do, more words to get down. The prospect doesn't depress me. I'm well aware of Aldo Leopold's warning that "one of the penalties of an ecological education is that one lives alone in a world of wounds." It is a world of wounds, but we are not alone. The solitary act of creative nonfiction writing leads to the second act of solidarity with readers who are willing to bear witness through the writer's words—who are then willing to act.

ACKNOWLEDGMENTS

These essays previously appeared in the following publications.

"Advice" from *Rough Likeness* © 2011 by Lia Purpura. Reprinted with the permission of The Permissions Company, Inc., on behalf of Sarabande Books, www.sarabandebooks.org.

"Getting 'Grip'" in *Fourth Genre* 11.2 (2009): 121–127.

"Grip" in *Fourth Genre* 11.2 (2009): 119–120.

"Night" in *The Mountain and the Fathers: Growing Up on the Big Dry* (Counterpoint, 2012) by Joe Wilkins. Copyright © 2012 by Joe Wilkins from *The Mountain and the Fathers*. Reprinted by permission of Counterpoint.

"Walking Home" is reprinted from *This Is Not the Ivy League: A Memoir*, by Mary Clearman Blew, by permission of the University of Nebraska Press. Copyright 2011 by the Board of Regents of the University of Nebraska.

CONTRIBUTORS

NANCER BALLARD, a writer of nonfiction, fiction, literary criticism, and poetry, is the recipient of a 2010 Tavris Grant from Brandeis University for her work on the role and experience of time in life and fiction, and is developing a series of multimedia presentations and essays on the role of time in literature, visual arts, music, and human experience. Her creative nonfiction has recently appeared in *Thema* and *South Street Review*. She is currently a Resident Scholar at Brandeis University's Women's Studies Research Center, and a practicing environmental lawyer. She has coauthored and served as a consultant on a children's supplemental textbook series combining mathematics and folktales, and has taught interdisciplinary courses in biology, psychology, and literature at Ithaca College. In addition to her work on time, Ms. Ballard is writing a creative nonfiction book that includes memoir, history, psychology, neurobiology, and the physiology of time and sensation.

H. LEE BARNES teaches creative writing at the College of Southern Nevada. In previous lives he was a soldier, a deputy sheriff, a casino dealer, a martial arts instructor, and a construction laborer. He is the author of eight books, two of which, *Dummy Up and Deal* and *When We Walked Above the Clouds*, are narrative nonfiction. His essays, social commentaries, and personal narratives reflecting his life experiences have appeared in literary journals and alternative publications. When not teaching or writing, he tours on his motorcycle or hikes the back trails of the Southwest with his springer spaniel.

KIM BARNES was born in Lewiston, Idaho, in 1958 and one week later returned with her mother to their small line-shack on Orofino Creek, where Barnes's father worked as a gyppo logger. The majority of her childhood was spent in the isolated settlements and cedar camps along the North Fork of Idaho's Clearwater River. Barnes's first memoir, *In the Wilderness: Coming of Age in Unknown Country*, received a PEN/Jerard Fund Award and a Pacific

Northwest Booksellers Award, and was a finalist for the Pulitzer Prize, as well as the PEN/Martha Albrand Award. Her second memoir, *Hungry for the World*, was a Borders Books New Voices Selection. She is the author of three novels: *Finding Caruso*; *A Country Called Home*, winner of the 2009 PEN Center USA Literary Award in Fiction, a Book-of-the-Month-Club Main Selection, and named a Best Book of 2008 by *The Washington Post*, *Kansas City Star*, and *The Oregonian*; and, most recently, *In the Kingdom of Men*, set in 1960s Saudi Arabia. Barnes is coeditor of two anthologies: *Circle of Women: An Anthology of Contemporary Western Women Writers*, edited with Mary Clearman Blew, and *Kiss Tomorrow Hello: Notes from the Midlife Underground by Twenty-Five Women Over Forty*, edited with Claire Davis. Her essays, poems, and stories have appeared and are forthcoming in a number of magazines and anthologies, including *The New York Times*, *WSJ Online*, *The Georgia Review*, *Shenandoah*, *Oprah Magazine*, *Good Housekeeping*, *MORE Magazine*, and the Pushcart Prize anthology. Barnes teaches at the University of Idaho and lives with her husband, the poet Robert Wrigley, on Moscow Mountain.

MARY CLEARMAN BLEW's most recent book is *This Is Not the Ivy League: A Memoir*. Her fiction collection, *Runaway*, won a Pacific Northwest Booksellers Award, as did her memoir *All But the Waltz: Essays on a Montana Family*. A novel, *Jackalope Dreams*, won the 2008 Western Heritage Award. She teaches creative writing at the University of Idaho and Pacific Lutheran University.

JOY CASTRO is the author of the memoir *The Truth Book*, the creative nonfiction collection *Island of Bones*, and the literary thrillers *Hell or High Water* and *Nearer Home*, and the editor of the collection *Family Trouble: Memoirists on the Hazards and Rewards of Revealing Family*. Her nonfiction has appeared in anthologies and in journals including *Seneca Review*, *Fourth Genre*, and *The New York Times Magazine*. She teaches literature, creative writing, and Latino studies at the University of Nebraska–Lincoln.

ROBIN HEMLEY is the author of ten books of nonfiction and fiction, most recently the short story collection *Reply All* and the craft meditation, *A Field Guide for Immersion Writing*. He's the recipient of many awards and honors, including three Pushcart Prizes, two in fiction and one in nonfiction, a Guggenheim Fellowship, The Nelson Algren Award for Fiction, and many more. He is a graduate of the Iowa Writers Workshop and a former fellow at The Fine Arts Work Center in Provincetown, and his work has appeared in many anthologies and journals including *The Southern Review, Ploughshares, The Sun, Orion, The Believer, McSweeney's Internet Tendency, The New York Times, The Wall Street Journal, New York Magazine, The Chicago Tribune*, and many others. He is the Founder of NonfictioNOW, a former editor of *The Bellingham Review*, and for nine years was Director of the Nonfiction Writing Program at the University of Iowa. He currently lives in Singapore where he directs the Writing Program and is Writer-in-Residence at Yale-NUS College.

JUDITH KITCHEN's latest book of essays is *Half in Shade: Family, Photography, Fate.* In addition, she has edited three collections of short nonfiction pieces for W. W. Norton. Her awards include two Pushcart Prizes in nonfiction. She lives in Port Townsend, Washington, and serves on the faculty of the Rainier Writing Workshop Low-Residency MFA at Pacific Lutheran University.

BRENDA MILLER is the author of *Listening Against the Stone, Blessing of the Animals, Season of the Body*, and coauthor of *Tell It Slant: Writing and Shaping Creative Nonfiction* and *The Pen and The Bell: Mindful Writing in a Busy World*. Her work has received six Pushcart Prizes and has been published in numerous journals. She is a Professor of English at Western Washington University and serves as Editor-in-Chief of the *Bellingham Review*.

ANDER MONSON is the author of five books, including *Vanishing Point* and *The Available World*, a website, a decoder wheel, two chapbooks, and other paraphernalia. The editor of the magazine *DIAGRAM* and the New Michigan Press, he lives and teaches in Tucson, Arizona.

DINTY W. MOORE is author of *The Mindful Writer: Noble Truths of the Writing Life,* as well as the memoir *Between Panic & Desire*, winner of the Grub Street Nonfiction Book Prize in 2009. A professor of nonfiction writing at Ohio University, Moore edits *Brevity*, an online journal of flash nonfiction, and lives in Athens, Ohio, where he grows heirloom tomatoes and edible dandelions.

SEAN PRENTISS is an Assistant Professor of English at Norwich University and the creative editor of *Backcountry Magazine*. His essays, poems, and stories have appeared in *Brevity, Passages North, Sycamore Review, ISLE, Spoon River, Nimrod,* and many other journals. He was recently named an Albert J. Colton Fellow by the Utah Humanities.

LIA PURPURA is the author of seven collections of essays, poems, and translations, including *Rough Likeness* (essays). Her awards include a 2012 Guggenheim Foundation Fellowship, Finalist for the National Book Critics Circle Award, NEA and Fulbright Fellowships, three Pushcart prizes, work in *Best American Essays 2011,* the AWP Award in Nonfiction, and the Beatrice Hawley, and Ohio State University Press awards in poetry. Recent work appears in *Agni, Field, The Georgia Review, Orion, The New Republic, The New Yorker, The Paris Review,* and elsewhere. She is Writer-in-Residence at the University of Maryland, Baltimore County, and teaches at the Rainier Writing Workshop.

ERIK REECE is the author of *An American Gospel: On Family, History, and the Kingdom of God* and *Lost Mountain: A Year in the Vanishing Wilderness,* which won Columbia University's John. B. Oakes Award for Distinguished Environmental Journalism and the Sierra Club's David R. Brower Award for Environmental Excellence. His work has appeared, in *Harper's, Orion, The Nation, The Oxford American, The New York Times,* and elsewhere. He is writer-in-residence at the University of Kentucky in Lexington, where he teaches environmental journalism, writing, and literature.

JONATHAN ROVNER was raised in the rugged suburbs of Centennial, Colorado. He teaches at Morehead State University.

BOB SHACOCHIS, the award-winning author of seven books, writes both fiction and nonfiction. His recent work includes a travel memoir, *Between Heaven and Hell,* and a novel, *The Woman Who Lost Her Soul.* He teaches at the graduate writing programs at Bennington and Florida State.

JOE WILKINS is the author of a memoir, *The Mountain and the Fathers: Growing up on the Big Dry,* a finalist for the 2013 *Orion* Book Award, and two collections of poems, *Notes from the Journey Westward,* winner of the 17th Annual White Pine Press Poetry Prize, and *Killing the Murnion Dogs,* a finalist for the Paterson Poetry Prize and the High Plains Book Award. His poems, essays, and stories have appeared in *The Georgia Review*, *The Missouri Review*, *The Southern Review*, *Ecotone*, *The Sun*, *Orion*, and *Slate*, among other magazines and literary journals. He lives with his wife, son, and daughter in western Oregon, where he teaches writing at Linfield College.